As Christ
Submits to the
Church

As Christ
Submits to the
Church

A Biblical Understanding of Leadership
and Mutual Submission

Alan G. Padgett

Baker Academic
a division of Baker Publishing Group
Grand Rapids, Michigan

Published by Baker Academic
a division of Baker Publishing Group
P.O. Box 6287, Grand Rapids, MI 49516-6287
www.bakeracademic.com

Printed in the United States of America

Library of Congress Cataloging-in-Publication Data
Padgett, Alan G., 1955–
    As Christ submits to the church : a biblical understanding of leadership and mutual submission / Alan G. Padgett.
      p.   cm.
    Includes bibliographical references (p.   ) and indexes.
    ISBN 978-0-8010-2700-0 (pbk.)
    1. Sex role—Biblical teaching. 2. Submissiveness—Biblical teaching. 3. Servant leadership—Biblical teaching. 4. Bible. N.T.—Theology. I. Title.
BS2545.S37P33 2011
220.8'3053—dc22
                                                2011005204

Unless otherwise indicated, Scripture quotations are the author's own translation.

Scripture quotations labeled NRSV are from the New Revised Standard Version of the Bible, copyright © 1989, by the Division of Christian Education of the National Council of the Churches of Christ in the United States of America. Used by permission. All rights reserved.

11   12   13   14   15   16   17   7   6   5   4   3   2   1

For Sally
My one and only
Song of Songs 8:6–7

Contents

Acknowledgments

O f the making of books there is no end," said the wise Preacher (Eccles. 12:12). After some decades of fits and starts, the writing of this book has come to a fruitful end, for which we are grateful to God. I want to thank my long-suffering editor Robert Hosack for approaching me in the first place and for his support and patience over the years. My thanks also go to B. J. Heyboer and Rodney Clapp of Baker Academic for their continued friendship and support.

I am very glad of the grace of God in calling me to be a professor at Luther Seminary. The community here is a wonderful place to teach, live, worship, and work at being a theologian. My thanks are due to many people who have helped see this book to its fruition over the years. These include our very talented faculty secretary, Victoria Smith, who read through the entire manuscript, made many helpful suggestions, and greatly revised the Scripture index. Likewise, my most excellent research assistant, Reverend Karin Craven, read over the book and created the indices. The Reverend Dr. Beth Johnson was also kind enough to read the whole book and make a number of critical remarks out of her expertise in New Testament and her experience as a pastor. Friends at church, including our pastor, Donna Martinson, and Mark Tondra, read portions of the book and made comments. Please accept my thanks to all of you. Finally, my wife, Dr. Sally Bruyneel, has been very kind and supportive. She is in her person a model of Christian leadership and sacrificial love. I would say more, but mere words will never be enough. In gratitude to the Lord, I dedicate this work to her.

Abbreviations

AB	Anchor Bible
ANF	*Ante-Nicene Fathers*
BDAG	Bauer, W., F. W. Danker, W. F. Arndt, and F. W. Gingrich. *A Greek-English Lexicon of the New Testament and Other Early Christian Literature*. 3rd ed. Chicago, 1999
CCSG	Corpus Christianorum: Series graeca. Turnhout, 1977–
CT	*Christianity Today*
Di	*Dialog*
EvQ	*Evangelical Quarterly*
FC	Fathers of the Church. Washington, DC, 1947–
ICC	International Critical Commentary
Int	*Interpretation*
JAAR	*Journal of the American Academy of Religion*
JBL	*Journal of Biblical Literature*
JETS	*Journal of the Evangelical Theological Society*
JSNT	*Journal for the Study of the New Testament*

JSNTSup Journal for the Study of the New Testament: Supplement
         Series

JTS   *Journal of Theological Studies*

KJV   King James Version

NICNT   New International Commentary on the New Testament

NIGTC   New International Greek Testament Commentary

NPNF[2]   *Nicene and Post-Nicene Fathers*, Series 2

NRSV   New Revised Standard Version

PNTC   Pillar New Testament Commentary

PriscPap *Priscilla Papers*

PTR   *Princeton Theological Review*

SC   Sources chrétiennes. Paris, 1943–

TDNT   *Theological Dictionary of the New Testament*. Edited by
          G. Kittel and G. Friedrich. Translated by G. W. Bromiley.
          10 vols. Grand Rapids, 1964–1976

ThTo   *Theology Today*

TJ   *Trinity Journal*

TynBul   *Tyndale Bulletin*

WBC   Word Biblical Commentary

ZEE   *Zeitschrift für evangelische Ethik*

Introduction

At the heart of this study of biblical, evangelical ethics is a basic question: Does Christ submit to the church, his body and bride? Does Jesus our Lord provide us with an example of submission to others, in which he calls us to follow? My answer will be yes, and I shall show from Scripture that this is the view of the New Testament in general. In giving a positive answer to this question, we need to distinguish between two types of submission. The first type (type I) comes from the realm of political and military struggle. This type of submission is obedience to an external authority, which can be voluntary but often is not. The second type of submission (type II) is one that comes from personal relationships and is often based on love or compassion. In this second type, submission is the *voluntary* giving up of power in order to take up the role of a slave, so that one may serve the needs of another person. The first type is external, hierarchical, and legal. The second type is internal, personal, and a kind of gift or grace. I will argue that Jesus submits to the church only in the second sense of the word. While those who follow Jesus may submit to the Lord in

the first sense to start with, a deeper discipleship will lead the
Christian toward the second, interpersonal type.

A second theme of our study will be the matter of gender
roles. Recent scholarship among fundamentalists and more conservative evangelicals has raised the issue of role relationships
between men and women. This debate is the occasion of my
thinking about this question from a biblical perspective. But I
now see that the question behind this book is in fact broader than
gender issues. When we comprehend the nature of discipleship
in general and the concrete character of the love extolled in the
Bible, we are in a better position to address the role relationships
of men and women from a consistent Christian understanding.
At the heart of this issue is the question of leadership. What
does it mean to be a *leader* who takes following Jesus seriously?
It is this larger question that we will pursue in this book, and
in the light of which we will examine what Scripture has to say
about male-female relationships.

We start with a consideration of the origin of this debate
among evangelicals and an overview of what it means to read
the Bible as the Word of God in evangelical thought. *Evangelical* in this book means having to do with the gospel of Jesus
Christ. I argue that evangelical theology will read the whole of
Scripture on any topic (a canonical sense) and not be satisfied
with the teaching of any part in isolation. We read the whole
of Scripture because we confess that Jesus is the Messiah of
Israel. This implies a concern not only for the original meaning of the text in its social and literary context (what I call the
conventional sense), but also for the text's meaning in the Bible
as a whole (canonical sense). This Christ-centered, canonical
sense of any biblical text is needed before we can rightly grasp
its authoritative meaning for life today (contemporary sense).
These arguments take us to the end of chapter 1.

I next consider the very idea of an ethics of roles. This is a
concept one finds used by so-called complementarian theolo-

gians, but they do not explore it very fully. Just what is a role, ethically? I argue that any ethic of roles necessarily involves time (narrative), character, and community. True, the way we live out some limited roles (say, being a lawyer) is external to a person's character. The role may tell us nothing about what the person is actually like, morally speaking. Other social roles (like being a parent) display the moral virtues or vices of the actor. I argue that gender roles are the latter type—that is, morally direct roles. The way we act out our gender roles shows the world what our character is like.

Having paved the way to consider Scripture, our study turns first to Jesus. In the Gospels we discover a consistent ethics of leadership, which also relies on the notion of a role. To be a leader, for Jesus, is to take up the role of a slave toward "the least of these." Those in power use that power not for their own gain or security, but radically give it away in love and service to the other, especially to the people they are leading. Jesus not only teaches this to his disciples, he models it in the washing of their feet.

The message, model, and ministry of Jesus set the framework for our reading of the New Testament letters, especially those of Paul. Rather than jump right to passages dealing with submission, we first look to the main epistles of Paul, the central letters where he sets forth his theology and ethics. These major letters are usually understood to include Romans, Galatians, 1–2 Corinthians, and Philippians. How does Paul teach us to treat one another in the body of Christ, which is the church? Given the teachings of Jesus in the Gospels, it is fascinating to see that Paul also adopts an ethics of roles. The Christian takes up the role of a slave in caring for one's sisters and brothers out of love for Christ, giving of ourselves for the glory of God and the edification of the church. This notion is found throughout his letters, for example, "We preach not ourselves, but Jesus Christ as Lord, and ourselves as your slaves for the sake of Jesus"

(2 Cor. 4:5). Also consider this text: "We who are strong ought to bear with the failings of the weak, and not please ourselves. Let each of us please our neighbor, for his or her own good, to build them up; for Christ did not please himself" (Rom. 15:1–3). There is a great deal of mutual care and regard, mutual service and ministry, in the Christian ethics in the major letters of Paul.

This leads us to a simple, practical conclusion. In terms of the ethics of roles, servant leadership and mutual submission are practically the same. Servant leadership is simply the ethics of mutual submission applied to those who are leaders. *All* Christians are in fact called to mutual regard, service, and care for one another. In the language of the New Testament, this translates into *taking up the role* of a servant or slave out of love for one's sister or brother. The expectation is that such roles are both temporary and mutual, not a social institution of strict hierarchy.

It is this larger ethics of mutual submission (type II submission) that we then see at work in the famous passage on marriage in Paul, Ephesians 5:21–33. A key to this text is the first sentence: "Submit yourselves one to another out of reverence for [or "fear of"] Christ" (Eph. 5:21). A study of this passage in light of what we have already learned about the ethics of Jesus and Paul clarifies what Paul is saying to husbands. They too are called to act like Jesus did when he washed the disciples' feet: they are to submit to their wives, when this submission is understood as taking up the role of a servant. Likewise, the wife is to submit to her husband. Certainly, there was a hierarchy at work, a Roman, pagan patriarchy that the Ephesians would have known well. Yet Paul's teachings, if taken to heart, would undermine this fixed hierarchy with a mutual submission between husband and wife. The gender roles of "husband" and "wife" are given a radical Christ-centered reorientation by the apostle and brought into line with the example of Christ's own type II submission to the church.

Having made this argument with respect to Ephesians 5, we then proceed to discuss other "submission" passages in 1 Corinthians, 1 Peter, and the Pastoral Epistles (1–2 Timothy, Titus). *Submission* is used in slightly different ways in each of these passages. They should not be lumped together, but each studied carefully. For example, in 1 Corinthians 14:33–36 we discover that talkative women are to be quiet in church and submit to the order of the worship service as led by the Holy Spirit. This is not a submission of wives to husbands or women to men in general terms. Rather, it is about decency and order in the worship service of the church.

It must also be said that in the later letters of the New Testament, for example in 1 Peter, the submission enjoined to wives and slaves is far less mutual, approaching a kind of type I submission, where the weak submit to the strong as a social institution. The missionary context of persecution in the Roman Empire goes some way toward explaining this transition, for the church had become quite concerned about the attitudes outsiders were taking toward the new religion. But the tension between the type I submission in 1 Peter and the mutual submission (type II) of Ephesians should not be overlooked.

The central argument of this book is to see these differences and prefer that consistent ethic of servant leadership and mutual submission that finds its center in the Gospels and the major letters of Paul. We should interpret and apply the ethics of submission in other, later letters in this larger canonical context. When we center our application of the New Testament ethics of submission on Jesus Christ and his teachings on leadership, we see that submission between men and women is a temporary part of our gender roles. This kind of self-giving out of love should be what every Christian owes to one another out of the fear of Christ. Such roles will always be temporary and mutual in the community of the church over time. This ethic does not support the view, so common in church tradition, of a fixed hierarchy of women always subordinate to men. In fact, the ethics of roles in the church that calls for mutual submission should undermine it.

In the final chapter of the book, we think about applying this biblical ethic of submission today. God's Word in Scripture calls forth not only works of love like mutual submission, but also the hunger and thirst for justice. Working together, love and justice guide the church and the Christian family into the wisdom of finding the right attitude and action in specific times and places. Seeking to serve one another in love, and taking up the role of a servant, is first of all an ethic for those who lead and are in power. Although often abused by those in power to prop up the status quo, this ethic should in fact be used to undermine oppression and injustice in the name of mutual submission.

1

Living Gospel

Evangelical Approaches to Gender Roles

O urs is a culture in which issues of gender and sexuality are confusing and conflicted, both within and outside of the Christian faith. As followers of Christ, we believe that the church has a message to carry forth into the world, and that this creates a context for understanding human embodiment. Christians should be in dialogue with our culture about sex and gender. The problem is that the church has her own struggles with how best to articulate the gospel in this area. Our own internal discussions of sex and gender have moved beyond the gracious and civil to the unruly and entrenched, leaving us without the essential composure to speak carefully to the world beyond. I wrote this book to help us reconsider our views within the Christian ethic of submission, especially in light of Scripture and the gospel.

The occasion of this reflection is the current debate within Christianity concerning gender roles, particularly those in the

1

church and home. Even believers who follow Christ Jesus, seeking to know and love God with all they are, respecting the authority of Scripture as the Word of God, can be confused or
in conflict. Those who are sure about the "right" answers are
often in conflict with like-minded people in their own churches
who disagree. What's going on? The simple answer one sometimes hears makes appeal to "worldly" or pagan philosophies:
worldly thinking has misled Christians into misunderstanding
the Word of God. Frankly, this answer simply does not fit the
facts; and in any case, it cuts both ways. The viewpoint I will
call "man-centered leadership," also known as complementarian
theology, has its roots not purely in Scripture but in the patriarchal philosophies of Greece and Rome, passed on in Christian circles even unto the present generation. What passes for
"traditional" views on the role relationships of men and women
is often nothing more than the Bible mixed with Victorian attitudes concerning gender. This is a modern development and
does not come from Scripture itself.

Evangelical scholars have used a great deal of ink and paper
in the debates on this topic since the 1970s. This book will take
a new approach in the hope of mounting a convincing argument
that man-centered, top-down leadership is neither biblical nor
evangelical. A biblical ethic that is Christ-centered and truly
evangelical is not concerned with issues of gender but with
power. Specifically, the question is this: how shall disciples of
Jesus use the power they have in social situations? "Power" here
includes the powers we have by virtue of our social status. Our
answer will be a basic one: the Christian leader is one who takes
up the role of a servant, just as Jesus did. This is simply what
mutual submission means. *Mutual submission is the concrete
action of Christian love working within the social structures
of this world.*

It is not uncommon among evangelicals to focus on interpreting four or five sections of Scripture as the source for a particu-

lar take on gender roles. Though we will look to exegesis, we will not be looking only to particular portions of biblical text. Pure exegesis alone cannot solve this debate. Issues of men and women and leadership involve a much larger, Christian understanding of ethics, biblical interpretation, and philosophy of ministry. To start, we will take a brief historical overview of the recent debate to get a broader perspective on where folks have staked a claim theologically. Then we will look at what it means to be an evangelical leader and theologian. Are there specific implications and obligations that come when one assumes that mantle? Finally, this opening chapter will consider what it means to read the whole Bible as an evangelical, Christ-centered disciple.

The Recent Debate among Evangelicals

The debate on gender has been going on among American evangelical theologians for over thirty years now, though at times it feels that the strident tone in some quarters has gone on *hundreds* of years too long. Whether it intrigues or wears on those of us in the evangelical community, it shows no sign of resolution or diminution.[1] If we are to engage in genuine dialogue rather than oppositional posturing and prooftexting, it is important to gain a lay of the land. Toward this end, I invite your attention to a brief overview that sets out the main issues in the current

1. For an overview of this debate by a participant on the egalitarian side, see Ronald W. Pierce, "Contemporary Evangelicals for Gender Equality," in *Discovering Biblical Equality: Complementarity without Hierarchy*, ed. Ronald W. Pierce and Rebecca Merrill Groothuis (Downers Grove, IL: InterVarsity, 2004), 58–75. For a book-length study, see Pamela Cochran, *Evangelical Feminism: A History* (New York: New York University Press, 2004). A useful and well-researched survey of the current situation for women evangelical scholars is provided by Nicola H. Creegan and Christine D. Pohl, *Living on the Boundaries: Evangelical Women, Feminism, and the Theological Academy* (Downers Grove, IL: InterVarsity, 2005). They demonstrate the continuing struggles women face in the American evangelical subculture, even among the highly educated.

debate. Since this book is concerned with evangelical theology and ministry, some understanding of the current debate among evangelical scholars is helpful in setting the stage for our work. A short look back at recent debates will make it clear where the argument presented here fits into the larger conversation concerning gender, leadership, and the ethic of roles.

Roots of the Conflict

The traditional view of the church on women is usually well known by those with a seminary education. Books like *The Church and the Second Sex* (1968) by Mary Daly chronicle the sad story of Christian patriarchy.[2] While there are differences in detail, the traditional theological view is simply that women should not take up leadership roles in the church or society because they are inadequate or even defective in some ways by their very nature. How they are defective differs from theologian to theologian. Sometimes women were thought to be less rational than men, moved by emotion rather than a higher reflective capacity. Another and sometimes tandem misrepresentation is that the female is a lesser reflection of the full image of God as found in the first-created male. Still others look to physical form as indicative of inferior capacities. Perhaps women's bodily powers (which include a passive role in procreation) are less active or potent. Sometimes women's souls have been portrayed as fully instantiated versions of the more easily tempted Eve, who also possesses the contradictory capacity of being so clever that she can subvert male rationality and lead him into sin.

The point is that, for traditional Christian patriarchy, some *ontological* reason having to do with the way things are "by nature" exists to ground the submission of women and their exclusion from the priesthood. I mention this to make plain

2. Daly published a paperback edition "with a new feminist postchristian intro-duction" in 1975 with Harper & Row (New York, 1975).

that most American evangelicals and fundamentalists today hold to some kind of role-hierarchy for women that is *nontra-ditional*. It is as much a revision of the mainstream traditions of the church as either biblical equality or Christian feminism. But getting to this so-called complementarian perspective will require a short tour of the history of theology as a background to current debates.

Ever since the Reformation, women and men have been argu-ing on the grounds of Scripture and right reason that women can be called to ministry and gifted by the Spirit just like men. No doubt this argument was itself grounded in common Reforma-tion teachings like the priesthood of all believers and justification by faith alone based on the work of Christ (not on our own merits or "natures"). Women in the Magisterial Reformation made such arguments rather early on. Argula von Grumbach (née von Stauffer; 1492–1554) is an excellent example.[3] In the Radical Reformation, many voices, such as the Quaker leader Margaret Fell Fox (1614–1702), were at the forefront of arguing from Scripture and right reason that women should be given access to ministry roles long reserved for male privilege. Her 1667 book *Women's Speaking Justified, Proved and Allowed by Scripture* is an early tract on this topic—one of the first in English.[4]

But the debate did not end with a few voices in the Reforma-tion and post-Reformation centuries. In the evangelical move-ments of the nineteenth century too, women and men advocated an end to slavery and likewise a fuller place for Christian women in church and society. The lay theologian and popular preacher Phoebe Palmer (1807–74) is a good example of someone who

3. On her work see Peter Matheson, *Argula von Grumbach: A Woman's Voice in the Reformation* (Edinburgh: T&T Clark, 1995).
4. Conveniently reprinted in modern type and spelling in *A Sincere and Constant Love: An Introduction to the Work of Margaret Fell*, ed. T. H. S. Wallace (Richmond, IN: Friends United Press, 1992).

did this kind of work.[5] I mention these movements and voices only to point out that arguing for greater roles for women on biblical and Christian grounds is not a new phenomenon. It was not created *ex nihilo* out of the women's movement of the 1960s but perpetuates a centuries-long tradition in the church. But there is no doubt that the recent discussion among American evangelicals was stimulated by secular feminism during the middle decades of the twentieth century, even as secular feminist thought was stimulated and nurtured by earlier Christian movements for the equality of women in the nineteenth century.[6] Still, if we carry one thing forward from here, it is this: the argument of this book is not grounded in feminist theory. We are concerned first with biblical study and ethics, especially with the ethic of loving service and submission—a topic many feminists would reject out of hand. Thus, our study is not a kind of Christian feminism, but rather an evangelical investigation of a biblical ethic of mutual submission.

Recent Debates over Scripture

The current debates have their roots in the rise of neoevangelical thought from the fundamentalist movement. The term *fundamentalist* here is not intended to invoke any pejorative connotations. In this book, *fundamentalist* is used in its best sense, describing a movement in American religion that was a reaction to modernism and liberal theology. In the early period following World War II, fundamentalist scholars began to reengage the larger culture from a biblical perspective. The emergence of more open fundamentalist thought after the war created the "neoevangelical" movement and, along with it, cen-

5. See her book on this topic: Phoebe Palmer, *The Promise of the Father* (Boston: Degan, 1859).

6. For an overview of the nineteenth-century debate and its Christian roots, see S. Wilkens and A. G. Padgett, *Christianity and Western Thought*, vol. 2, *A History of Philosophers, Ideas, and Movements* (Downers Grove, IL: InterVarsity, 2000), 209–15.

tral American evangelical institutions like *Christianity Today* magazine, the National Association of Evangelicals, and Fuller Theological Seminary.[7] Typical of fundamentalists before this period was the traditional view surveyed above—that is, basing the submission of women on their "natural" inferiority.

An example of this view can be seen in *The Place of Women in the Church*, a book written by fundamentalist Bible scholar C. C. Ryrie of Dallas Theological Seminary. In it he points out places where the spiritual role of women was "elevated," for example, by Jesus in the Gospels. He insisted that subordination is entirely different from subjection or inferiority. Yet he also argued from 1 Corinthians 11:8–9 that "the position of the woman is a secondary one because she was created out of the man. The Christian doctrine of order in creation involving subordination requires the Christian practice of manifesting that order in public worship."[8] Unlike participants in the evangelical debates that spark our study in this book, Ryrie and others within the fundamentalist movement all but assured that among them the issue of submission of women was for the most part a closed matter. Things were soon to change for the neoevangelicals, however, in response to other voices within that movement.

Stimulated in part by the women's movement of the 1960s, some American evangelical scholars began to argue on a number of fronts—including biblical interpretation—for the full equality of women in the church, home, and society. Calling their view "biblical feminism" to distinguish it from Christian

7. For an overview of the rise of neoevangelical leaders out of fundamentalism, with a focus on Calvinism and Fuller Seminary, see George Marsden, *Reforming Fundamentalism: Fuller Seminary and the New Evangelicalism* (Grand Rapids: Eerdmans, 1987); see also the collected work, Martin E. Marty, ed., *Fundamentalism and Evangelicalism* (Munich: K. G. Saur, 1993); and the recent monograph by Mark Noll, *American Evangelical Christianity: An Introduction* (Oxford: Blackwell, 2001).

8. C. C. Ryrie, *The Place of Women in the Church* (New York: Macmillan, 1958), 74. Later in this book we will study 1 Corinthians 11:2–16 in detail and reject Ryrie's claim.

feminism and feminism in general, these authors—both women and men—were at pains to put forward a new hermeneutic for the interpretation of the Bible regarding the place of women in church, home, and society. By all accounts, the first major book on this topic by neoevangelicals was Letha Scanzoni and Nancy Hardesty's *All We're Meant to Be: A Biblical Approach to Women's Liberation.*[9] Although written for a wide audience, the book's strength lies in the wide range of areas it considers, including hermeneutics, biblical interpretation, church history, and ethical matters of daily life. The subtitle's reference to "women's liberation" shows the influence of the women's movement in this significant early work, but the substance of the biblical and theological arguments is decisively evangelical.

Later defenders of biblical feminism would tone down the references to the feminist movement and speak in more neutral terms of *biblical equality*. Scholarly tomes like Paul K. Jewett's *Man as Male and Female* and more popular books like Virginia Ramey Mollenkott's *Women, Men, and the Bible* or Patricia Gundry's *Woman Be Free!* would press this view home in a variety of ways.[10] The Evangelical Women's Caucus (a task force within Evangelicals for Social Action) was organized during the 1970s when this new perspective was being developed, and helped promote the cause of women's equality on biblical, evangelical grounds.[11] While this position remained a minority voice within American evangelicalism, there were enough scholars and church leaders involved on the side of biblical equality to spark serious, though occasionally acrimonious, debate in evangelical circles.

9. Waco: Word, 1974. Two revisions were published later; the third edition was published by Eerdmans (Grand Rapids, 1993).

10. P. K. Jewett, *Man as Male and Female: A Study in Sexual Relationships from a Theological Point of View* (Grand Rapids: Eerdmans, 1975); V. R. Mollenkott, *Women, Men, and the Bible* (Nashville: Abingdon, 1977); Patricia Gundry, *Woman Be Free! The Clear Message of Scripture* (Grand Rapids: Zondervan, 1977).

11. On the Evangelical Women's Caucus, see the website of the Evangelical and Ecumenical Women's Caucus, http://www.eewc.org.

At this early stage, most of the discussion surrounded biblical interpretation. The primary source of engagement was the New Testament, especially key passages such as Luke 8:1–3; 1 Corinthians 11:2–16; 14:34–36; Ephesians 5:21–33; Galatians 3:28; and 1 Timothy 2:8–15, though the discussion did include a healthy amount of attention to Genesis 1–3. We will likewise study many of these texts later in this volume. While scholars differed in their approach to details, the overall message of biblical egalitarian scholarship was an attempt to reread the biblical texts in the light of a Christian ethics of love, a theology of mutual regard and dignity for all people, women and men, and the biblical idea of the unity of all believers in Christ. In part because of their shared tradition of biblical primacy, this group of scholars addressed the submission passages as earnestly and mindfully as any other evangelical group, subjecting texts to careful hermeneutical and exegetical analysis. As a result, they were often able to provide new interpretations that represented the best in evangelical faith and scholarship, yet that limited in some degree the universal scope of the demand for women and slaves to submit to their masters/husbands.

As the debate matured, those defending a man-centered view of leadership replied to this challenge with their own equally earnest arguments, including both popular and scholarly publications. An early and important study was by the New Testament scholar George W. Knight, *The New Testament Teaching on the Role Relationship of Men and Women*, published in 1977.[12] Here for the first time in print (at least that I have been able to discover), a conservative evangelical scholar argues that women and men are *equal* in being but that their *roles* are dif-

12. Grand Rapids: Baker Books, 1977. This book develops earlier essays, "Male and Female Related He Them," *CT* 20 (April 9, 1976): 13–17, and "The New Testament Teaching on the Role Relationship of Male and Female with Special Reference to the Teaching/Ruling Functions in the Church," *JETS* 18, no. 2 (Spring 1975): 81–91. A new edition appeared in 1985 titled *The Role Relationship of Men and Women: New Testament Teaching* (Chicago: Moody).

ferent. In the roles they take at home and in church, Knight
argues, women should submit to men; but the traditional idea
that this is somehow due to the inferior nature of women is appropriately rejected. This popular view, which we have earlier
identified as complementarian, is fairly young. It has also been
the source for the most current male-headship arguments and,
regrettably, some of the most acerbic.

For the purposes of our dialogue here, we should notice that
this view is no older on the historical evidence than about 1975.
Though it makes a number of claims to be the true expression
of historical Christian teachings, the historical evidence tells us
otherwise. Complementarian theology is just as revisionist, just
as influenced by modern thought, as the egalitarian view it paints
as new and unbiblical. In any case, the popularity of this perspective can be traced to a well-known collection, *Recovering
Biblical Manhood and Womanhood: A Response to Evangelical
Feminism* (1991), edited by John Piper and Wayne Grudem.[13] A
few years before this book was published, the Council on Biblical Manhood and Womanhood (CBMW) was formed. Their
interest goes beyond the exegetical to the political and ethical: to
opposing feminism and winning the day for what they perceive to
be "biblical" family values. We will argue in this work that such
values are not biblical but patriarchal—including the submission of women to husbands/fathers/male senior pastors in the
home and in church.[14] Though a number of these fundamentalist
and conservative evangelical leaders produce sound scholarship,
some—and CBMW in particular—often use a rhetorical hot but-
ton that plays on the cultural backlash against secular feminism.
They continue to insist that biblical equality and its proponents
represent a kind of "feminism"—this despite the fact that many,
if not most, evangelicals who embrace an egalitarian hermeneutic
reject the label "Christian feminism" to describe their view.

13. Wheaton: Crossway, 1991.
14. See more about CBMW at their website: http://www.cbmw.org.

The dynamics of the American fundamentalist and evangelical movement gave rise to its own biblical equality movement. Representative of the divergence in views of evangelicals themselves, there would be a split in the Evangelical Women's Caucus around 1988. Many leaders in this group wanted to embrace Christian feminism and gay rights more fully. In 1990 the group changed its name to Evangelical and Ecumenical Women's Caucus. The more conservative and biblically oriented members founded a new group, Christians for Biblical Equality (CBE), an organization that continues to argue for sexual and racial equality based on biblical principles.[15] CBE organized a massive, multiauthored response to *Recovering Biblical Manhood and Womanhood* titled *Discovering Biblical Equality: Complementarity without Hierarchy* (2004).[16] While this volume is instructive and interesting, the war of words within evangelical circles continues apace, with no side mounting a convincing win.

Role-hierarchy ("complementarity") continues to be strongest among fundamentalists and a majority of American evangelicals. There is a long way to go before most pastors and church leaders who call themselves "evangelical" will accept biblical equality as a legitimate alternative to their own viewpoint. At the same time, a number of evangelicals are convinced by the arguments for biblical equality on textual and hermeneutical grounds. Even deeply conservative evangelical theologians like Roger Nicole, Rebecca Merrill Groothuis, and Douglas Groothuis have embraced the biblical egalitarian perspective. What this shows, at its best, is that evangelicals are an engaged people, deeply committed to discerning and living what is true. In that same spirit, the goal of this larger study of biblical ethics and Christ-centered mutual submission is to set out for readers the strength and wisdom of the biblical egalitarian perspective.

15. See more about CBE at their website: http://www.cbeinternational.org.
16. Edited by Ronald Pierce and Rebecca Merrill Groothuis (Downers Grove, IL: InterVarsity, 2004).

The Turn to the Trinity

As a longtime systematic theologian, I have found a new twist in this debate very interesting: the turn to the Trinity. Complementarian scholars began to use the Trinity as a model for explicating and supporting their new view. At first glance this turn seems appropriate. After all, ecumenical and orthodox theology teaches that Jesus is equal in divinity to God the Father, yet the New Testament clearly teaches that in his role as savior and Messiah, he is submissive to the One he called *Abba*. But in order to fit the patriarchal model of women's submission into the new complementarian thinking, such submission on the part of the Son of God *could not be temporary*. The reason for this is that egalitarian scholars have argued for mutual submission between husband and wife in a Christian home as a vision of biblical equality. In such mutual submission, an ethic of submission is not so much rejected altogether (à la feminism) as it is limited by love, justice, and circumstance. Sometimes a husband will submit to his wife, or vice versa, depending on the context. Thus, a *temporary* submission of the Son models egalitarian ethics, not complementarian views.

Because of this teaching about mutual submission, the patriarchal theologians of the CBMW cannot allow that the submission of Jesus was temporary. Instead, they argue for an *eternal submission* of the Son to the Father. This submission is "functional" because the Son is of one being with the Father, but eternal because of these theologians' hierarchical model of submission. The persuasive power of complementarian theology can be seen in an example from Australia. The conservative evangelical Diocese of Sydney (Anglican) in 1999 commissioned a statement on the Trinity that taught, among other things, that the functional submission of the Son reflects "the eternal relationship between the persons of the Trinity"; it concluded that "unity, equality and subordination characterize the life of the Trinity."[17] This viewpoint is not in fact orthodox, and the report never became official doctrine. The reason is simple: the early church rejected the heresy of the eternal subordination of the Son in the Trinity, calling it "subordinationism." It is a development of the old Arian heresy in which Jesus is divine but not fully one with God the Father.

If with the church over the centuries we really affirm that there is one and only one God, how can there be enough separation between Father and Son for any kind of "submission" to even make sense? As Rebecca Merrill Groothuis points out, "Christian orthodoxy affirms that God and Christ are of the same substance and nature; they are not just equal in being but *one* in being."[18]

Due to the serious debates the 1999 statement sparked in Australia, it is perhaps no surprise that the foremost expert on this point of contention is the Australian theologian and pastor Kevin Giles. Giles has published two books arguing against the role-hierarchy position and in favor of orthodox trinitarian theology and biblical equality.[19] Drawing on careful biblical and historical scholarship, his arguments are both solid and convincing. One might think that this would be the end of things and that complementarians would back down, but this has not been the case. Instead, the CBMW and its scholars continue to insist on a "functional-eternal" submission of the Son to the Father.

17. "The Doctrine of Trinity and Its Bearing on the Relationship of Men and Women," a report from the Doctrine Commission of the Diocese of Sydney, reprinted as an appendix in Kevin Giles, *The Trinity and Subordinationism: The Doctrine of God and the Contemporary Gender Debate* (Downers Grove, IL: InterVarsity, 2002), quoting 127.

18. R. M. Groothuis, "'Equal in Being, Unequal in Role': Exploring the Logic of Woman's Subordination," in Pierce and Groothuis, *Discovering Biblical Equality*, 329 (emphasis in the original).

19. Giles, *The Trinity and Subordinationism*; and *Jesus and the Father: Modern Evangelicals Reinvent the Doctrine of the Trinity* (Grand Rapids: Zondervan, 2006).

Remarks and Reflections

As a Christian and a theologian, I confess that I find this ongoing debate both fascinating and educational. The continuing debates on matters of doctrine, hermeneutics, and exegesis between patriarchal and egalitarian evangelicals send one back to the texts of the church universal. Reading and rereading the ancient church creeds and other theological wrestlings helps hone one's own thinking in these areas. Here, I think, are a few lessons we can learn from these evangelical debates about gender roles that will be important for our current study. They have to do with the nature of biblical exegesis, the potential of Christian dialogue, and the capacity of Jesus Christ to speak to us—even us.

First, then, *careful biblical exegesis is an essential and happy obligation, but it is not enough*. The Bible is the Word of God and contains all things necessary for salvation. But the Bible does not always answer our contemporary questions. As we have already seen, those who wish to understand the complexities of this current conversation among evangelicals need to be aware of the issues surrounding key biblical texts. What we also have to understand is that more is at stake than exegesis alone. Exegesis is a critical reading and explanation of some portion of the biblical text. We do careful, close study of the words and look for context across the whole of the Bible. Yet we are not reading these texts for their own sake, and they do not come to us in a vacuum. Philosophical and theological issues in hermeneutics, including the influence of the natural and social sciences on biblical interpretation, must likewise be given careful consideration. Thus, exegesis alone does not yield biblical ethics.

Additionally, *evangelical scholars from all aspects of the intellectual spectrum—from committed conservative to quite progressive—can change their minds*. Another consideration is the need for patience with the progress of the Spirit and gentleness among Christians when we disagree. There is an understandable brashness and lack of gentleness in many an untested scholar, new to complicated ideas and unused to the frustrations of challenges to our ideas and ideals. It is the task of experienced scholars to model a more collegial regard toward those who disagree with us and with whom we disagree. For this reason, the sometimes dismissive attitudes and strident rhetoric in the debates of some "elder statesmen" in Christian leadership are sad and disappointing, and set the next generation off on the wrong foot. Good dialogue is possible, healthy debate does occur, and change can come. Thus, the fact that complementarian scholars have now come to accept the full equality and dignity of women is a sign of hope and a positive step, however small. Though they are likely to continue in their man-centered understanding of leadership, I am not ready yet to give up on this debate, as the present volume makes clear.

Finally, *we must always seek Jesus' face and voice in our efforts*. A consideration of the message, ministry, and teachings of Jesus Christ is just as relevant to the efforts of scholars as it is to any other person and can help us navigate the difficult waters surrounding this debate. The issues involved are admittedly complex, and questions of ethics and hermeneutics will need to be addressed; but it might be that here too a Christ-centered relational theology of love is a fruitful context for a fresh examination of the biblical evidence.

Living Gospel: What Is Evangelical Theology?

This book is a study in evangelical theology, in particular an evangelical, biblical ethic of mutual submission. But what is *evangelical* about theology? The word itself gives us a clue: evangelical theology is grounded in the gospel—that is, the good news about Jesus Christ. There is little general agreement on what counts as evangelical theology as distinct from evangelicalism as a histori-

cal movement within Christianity.[20] Many church historians have
accepted David Bebbington's argument that evangelicalism as a
movement in Anglo-American Christian history is characterized
by a focus on conversion, activism, biblical authority, and the
centrality of the cross.[21] Yet evangelical theology is not the same
as the evangelical movement in church history. Roman Catholics,
for example, can embrace an evangelical theology without becoming evangelical Protestants. Still, it is not hard to see in broad
strokes what evangelical theologians have in common, even when
any listing of such things will be diverse and disputed. We are
committed to Jesus Christ as savior and lord, fully human and
fully divine; we find the gospel most authoritatively articulated
in the Bible, which we confess to be the Word of God written
by human beings; we affirm the power of the gospel to forgive
sins and change lives, leading to discipleship and mission; and
we accept in general terms the orthodox, historic witness of the
church.[22] Evangelical theology is often contrasted with other
forms of Protestant thought. In particular, it is different from

20. For an argument that evangelical theology is multiform, see William J. Abraham, *The Coming Great Revival: Recovering the Full Evangelical Tradition* (New
York: Harper & Row, 1984).

21. See David W. Bebbington, "Evangelicalism in Its Settings: The British and
American Movements since 1940," in *Evangelicalism*, ed. Mark Noll, D. W. Bebbington, and G. A. Rawlyk (Oxford: Oxford University Press, 1991), 365–66; see also his
earlier monograph, *Evangelicalism in Modern Britain: A History from the 1730s to
the 1980s* (London: Unwyn Hyman, 1989).

22. For differing statements of what evangelical theology is about, see Donald
Bloesch, *Essentials of Evangelical Theology* (New York: Harper & Row, 1978),
1:7–22; David Edwards and John Stott, *Evangelical Essentials: A Liberal-Evangelical
Dialogue* (Downers Grove, IL: InterVarsity, 1988); Robert K. Johnston, "American
Evangelicalism: An Extended Family," in *The Variety of American Evangelicalism*,
ed. D. W. Dayton and R. K. Johnston (Knoxville: University of Tennessee Press,
1991); and Stanley Grenz, *Renewing the Center: Evangelical Theology in a Post-
theological Era*, 2nd ed. (Grand Rapids: Baker Academic, 2006), 214–25. For an
extended overview, see Roger Olson, *The Westminster Handbook to Evangelical
Theology* (Louisville: Westminster John Knox, 2004), 3–66, and note his comment
on page 3: "In this [broad] sense, then, evangelical is contrasted with moralistic or
legalistic religion; Evangelicalism is the Christian movement proclaiming the good
news that human persons can be saved by receiving a free gift won for them by Jesus
Christ in his death and resurrection."

fundamentalism, from liberal Protestant thought, and from many types of what was once called "neo-orthodoxy."

I believe that all the key elements of evangelical theology in the simple terms just described can be found in the Scriptures, especially when we make Jesus Christ the center of our reading of the Old and New Testaments.[23] This way of reading Scripture implies that the key confession of Christian faith is that Jesus is the Messiah and thus the Savior of the world. The very fact that we read together the Hebrew Bible and Greek Testament as one book is an implicit confession of faith that Jesus is the Messiah of Israel. This common evangelical confession, which is one with classic Christian faith, leads us to an important question for the current study: How should evangelicals approach the Bible? How do we read the Bible as the Word of God for Christian discipleship today? This question is obviously important for anyone who seeks to understand Christian leadership and gender roles from a solid foundation in biblical truth.

Reading the Bible as a Christian: Gospel-Centered Is Christ-Centered

The authority of Scripture is a central tenet of the Christian faith in general and of the evangelical or Reformation tradition in particular. Right back to the days of Martin Luther, evangelical Christians have focused on Scripture as the Word of God, the primary source and norm of Christian life and thought—and so of the continuing reform of the church. The United Methodist Church, for example, teaches that "Scripture is the primary source and criterion for Christian doctrine."[24] The Formula of

23. To develop this point further would take us too far from the current topic. For one short and readable guide to the basics, see John Stott, *Basic Christianity* (Grand Rapids: Eerdmans, 1971).

24. United Methodist Publishing House, *The Book of Discipline of The United Methodist Church, 2008* (Nashville: United Methodist Publishing House, 2008), par. 104.

Concord says it for Lutherans: "Holy Scripture alone remains the only judge, rule, and guiding principle, according to which, as the only touchstone, all teachings should and must be recognized and judged, whether they are good or evil, correct or incorrect."[25] While both European and American evangelicals have held the Bible as our highest written authority for faith and practice, there has been a great deal of debate concerning the nature and extent of this authority.

The authority question includes the character of the text as both inspired by God the Spirit and written by human beings as well as the proper approach to the interpretation of Scripture. We will focus here primarily upon the latter item: What does an evangelical theological hermeneutic look like? What does it mean to read and apply the Bible today as an evangelical? Or we might ask, what is the evangelical "grammar" for theological hermeneutics today?

In what follows, I will develop a threefold sense of Scripture for evangelical theology. This threefold sense is fairly straightforward: (1) conventional sense, (2) canonical sense, and (3) contemporary sense.[26] The fundamental and basic sense of Scripture is the conventional or "literal" sense. But this sense alone is insufficient. We accept the canon, in part, because of our faith in Christ and our historical attachment to the early church, which gave shape to our community of faith. So we are committed theologically to reading these books as canonical Scripture. Yet that commitment already changes the meaning of these texts from their conventional sense toward a larger meaning in the Christian Bible—what I call the canonical sense. The third sense, the contemporary sense, is one of application. These various senses are not steps or some kind of logical order; rather, they

25. *The Book of Concord: The Confessions of the Evangelical Lutheran Church*, ed. Robert Kolb and Timothy J. Wengert (Minneapolis: Fortress, 2000), 487.

26. See A. G. Padgett, "The Three-fold Sense of Scripture," in *Semper Reformandum: Studies in Honour of Clark H. Pinnock*, ed. S. E. Porter and A. R. Cross (Carlisle, UK: Paternoster, 2003), 275–88.

are constantly in dialogue with one another. The second or canonical sense of Scripture will be the focus of my attention here, but we will start with the conventional.

The Conventional Sense of Scripture

The first or conventional sense is basic, even foundational, to the other two. *Conventional sense* is my term for the plain, historical, or literal sense of Scripture, which is a common basis for communal discernment regarding the theological reading of Scripture in the church. We can share in common this most basic and foundational textual sense with believers and non-Christians, if only because it can be recovered through careful historical and linguistic research. But the meaning of Scripture for theology cannot be limited to this first sense. In this assertion I am going counter to many evangelical theologians, past and present, who find the mind or intention of the biblical author to be the limit of scriptural meaning for today. To take just one recent example, Ben Witherington claims in his recent book *The Problem with Evangelical Theology* that "hermeneutical principle #1" is "what the text could not have possibly meant to the original inspired biblical author, it cannot possibly mean today."[27]

Now this position does represent the understanding of the previous century on what creates meaning in a text. But almost no scholars who investigate the issue of meaning in texts now agree with this older view. Whether he knows it or not, Witherington's imagination is held captive to an *authorial hermeneutic*, in which the inner thoughts of the original author determine all possible future meanings for the text. This principle has been roundly criticized for many decades. There are two hermeneutical problems with it. The first is that we have no common ac-

---

27. Ben Witherington III, *The Problem with Evangelical Theology: Testing the Exegetical Foundations of Calvinism, Dispensationalism, and Wesleyanism* (Waco: Baylor University Press, 2005), x.

cess to the inner thoughts of the original biblical authors and editors. We cannot retrieve the inner subjective thoughts of an author deceased two millennia ago. The mind of the original author simply cannot become for us a criterion for judging what the text means.

Some have sought to avoid this problem by speaking of authorial intention as an objective, structural speech-act that creates the text as public discourse. Meir Sternberg has called this the "embodied" or "objectified" intention, and it is something we do have access to historically.[28] This objective intention sets the stage for what I am calling the conventional sense of the text. The sense of the text is fixed by the linguistic conventions of a time period and community and can be recovered by literary and historical research with some degree of likelihood. So far, so good.

But the second problem is a deeper, theological one. Objectively speaking, any individual text you and I read is placed by Christian theology within the context of the Bible as a whole. No biblical author is likely to have sat down at his or her desk and said, "Today I am going to write a chapter for the Bible." The Bible is a composite of the later church. So, by putting the whole Bible together and reading it as a unity, we are already going beyond anything that could have been in the mind and intention of any individual author or redactor. We must conclude that Witherington's "hermeneutical principle #1" should be rejected by Christians who read the whole Bible together as one book. This larger context changes the meaning and significance of particular texts within the Scriptures.

28. Meir Sternberg, *The Poetics of Biblical Narrative: Ideological Literature and the Drama of Reading* (Bloomington: Indiana University Press, 1985), 8–9. I owe this reference to Ben Ollenburger. See further the philosophical work of Nicholas Wolterstorff, *Divine Discourse: Philosophical Reflections on the Claim That God Speaks* (Cambridge: Cambridge University Press, 1995), and Ben Ollenburger's discussion of it in "Pursuing the Truth of Scripture," in *But Is It All True? The Bible and the Question of Truth*, ed. Alan G. Padgett and Patrick R. Keifert (Grand Rapids: Eerdmans, 2006), 44–65.

The Canonical Sense of Scripture

We are speaking in the previous paragraph of what I would call the canonical sense of Scripture. The gospel itself demands a "spiritual" or fuller sense of the Scriptures that goes beyond the conventional sense. The church of Jesus Christ cannot be content merely with a historical-literal reading of the text. Why? If the claims we make about Jesus at the heart of the gospel are true, then we can no longer approach the Bible in a way that limits us to what a given book's author might have originally thought. Jesus is the Messiah, the Christ. The church proclaims that he is also the Savior of the world and the Word of God made flesh. If these basic gospel elements are in fact true, then we need to reinterpret the entire history and testimony of Israel. If Jesus really is Savior, incarnate Word, and Messiah, then the whole of the Hebrew Bible needs to be read in a new light—the light of Christ. This is what the apostles themselves did, probably following the practice of their Lord (e.g., Luke 4:16–22).[29]

The gospel message is the basis of our canon of Scripture. The Old Testament was the Bible of Jesus and the earliest Christians. The Father of our Lord Jesus Christ is the Holy One of Israel, the God of the Old Testament. While some early Christian heretics such as Marcion rejected this conclusion, the identification of the God of Israel with the Father of our Lord Jesus Christ lies at the heart of the claim that Jesus is the Messiah of Israel. Jesus really is the Christ, the Messiah of Israel, and therefore his Father is the God of Israel. At the same time, the books of the New Testament look back to the life and teachings of Jesus and help us reread the Old Testament in the light of the Messiah. These books were accepted by the Christian community of faith as providing authentic witness to their risen Savior. As we noted earlier, to accept the Bible as a single book, then, is

29. On the historical character of this passage, see I. H. Marshall, *Commentary on Luke*, NIGTC (Grand Rapids: Eerdmans, 1978), 178–80; John Nolland, *Luke 1–9:20*, WBC (Dallas: Word, 1989), 192–95.

already to affirm the church's faith in Jesus as Messiah.[30] It is already to read the text of and for the community of faith in a way that must go beyond the original intention of the inspired author/editor.

While we thus need a fuller, canonical sense to rightly understand the Scriptures as evangelicals, the conventional sense of Scripture ought to be the basis and guide for any further spiritual or canonical sense. The conventional sense provides a common basis for any critique of fuller interpretations. In this insistence, we are in fact following the great doctors of the church, if not always in their practice then at least in their stated aims. The priority of the historical is no surprise in a historical religion whose God is at work in history. The story of God in the Bible is rooted and grounded in history—in exodus, exile, return, incarnation, crucifixion, and resurrection. As Diodore of Tarsus once wrote, "History [the literal sense] is not opposed to *theoria* [the spiritual sense]. On the contrary, it proves to be the foundation and basis of the higher senses."[31] Even Origen could call the historical meaning the "foundation" for any higher or spiritual sense.[32]

There has been a great deal of discussion about a "canonical" approach to biblical theology since the publication of B. S. Childs's stimulating work *Biblical Theology in Crisis*.[33] Childs

30. So, rightly, B. S. Childs, *Biblical Theology of the Old and New Testaments: Theological Reflection on the Christian Bible* (Minneapolis: Fortress, 1992), 80: "Although the church adopted from the synagogue a concept of scripture as an authoritative collection of sacred writings, its basic stance toward its canon was shaped by its christology. The authority assigned to the apostolic witnesses derived from their unique testimony to the life, death and resurrection of Jesus Christ."

31. Diodore of Tarsus, "Prologue" (CCSG 6:7). English translation in *Biblical Interpretation in the Early Church*, ed. Karlfried Froehlich (Minneapolis: Fortress, 1984), 85.

32. Origen uses the metaphor "foundation" for the historical sense in, for example, discussing Noah's ark. See Origen, *Homiliae in Genesim* 2.6 (SC 7:106–8; FC 71). See further Karen Jo Torjesen, *Hermeneutical Procedure and Theological Method in Origen's Exegesis* (Berlin: de Gruyter, 1985), 68: "Origen defines the particular referent of the literal sense differently and very precisely for each book or exegetical genre. The spiritual sense then flows naturally from this definition."

33. Philadelphia: Westminster, 1970.

and his colleague Hans Frei were both influenced in this direction by the biblical-theological work of Karl Barth. In light of the critics of this approach, I need to make clear from the outset that a canonical sense of Scripture is an explicitly Christian undertaking, based on faith.[34] I am not speaking of just any exegesis, but the theological and spiritual interpretation of the Bible by the community of faith.[35] My approach here is from faith to faith and concerns the fully theological understanding of the Bible for the Christian community, which presumes already faith in Jesus Christ—that is to say, I am employing a Christian theological hermeneutics.[36]

Unlike some evangelical or postliberal theologians, I believe that the historical and academic approach to the Bible is a significant and lasting contribution of the Enlightenment to the Christian faith.[37] We want to appreciate the Bible for what it is, and that means taking seriously the human character of the Bible and its authors. Patient and scholarly work over generations within the academy has provided all of us with a far better understanding of the nature, origin, and background of the various biblical writings. My own appreciation of the

34. For one important critic of Childs, see James Barr, *The Concept of Biblical Theology: An Old Testament Perspective* (Minneapolis: Fortress, 1999).

35. In a vast sea of literature, one clear proposal on how the Bible should be used in Christian theology is G. O'Collins and D. Kendall, *The Bible for Theology: Ten Principles for the Theological Use of Scripture* (New York: Paulist Press, 1997). For a more developed approach, see Francis Watson, *Text, Church and World* (Edinburgh: T&T Clark, 1994), and *Text and Truth: Redefining Biblical Theology* (Edinburgh: T&T Clark, 1997). For a collection of essays that discusses the divide between systematic and biblical theology, see Joel Green and Max Turner, eds., *Between Two Horizons: Spanning New Testament Studies and Systematic Theology* (Grand Rapids: Eerdmans, 2000). My concern here is the use of the Bible by the believing community, which would also include the use of the Bible in Christian doctrine.

36. As Robert Wall correctly notes, "The most crucial move theological hermeneutics must make is to recover Scripture for its use in Christian worship and formation" ("Reading the Bible from within Our Traditions: The 'Rule of Faith' in Theological Hermeneutics," in Green and Turner, *Between Two Horizons*, 91).

37. Francis Watson (*Text and Truth*, 33–63) rightly warns against the "eclipse of history" in the work of some postliberal and/or narrative theologians.

scholar's role is evident. The problem is this: however much we honor the guild of biblical scholarship, however much we have learned over the years thanks to their efforts, the church has very different aims and purposes in reading the Holy Bible. These differing aims and purposes put biblical scholars in conflict with ordinary believers, for difference in purpose produces difference in method.

The Contemporary Sense of Scripture

My own study of the sciences has convinced me that not only meaning, but also method, follows the aim and purpose of an academic discipline. As Aristotle once remarked, "Clearly, it is equally foolish to accept probable reasoning from the mathematician and to demand scientific proof from a rhetorician."[38] Methods mirror aims, as several important philosophers of science in the last century have concluded. They have helped overturn the rationalist dream of an "exact scientific methodology" that would overcome all ambiguity, be used in every discipline worthy of the name, and present us with a unified system of nature.[39] The rationalistic dream of there being one and only one right way to read the Bible must be resisted by thoughtful Christians who value the love and knowledge of God above all things. The Christian community, with its goals of worship, discipleship, and witness, has very different aims from the academic community of the Bible scholar. The Christian community, as a spiritual fellowship in search of the truth as it is embodied in

38. Aristotle, *Nicomachean Ethics* 1.13.1094B.

39. Particularly important in this regard was the work of Pierre Duhem, N. R. Hanson, Michael Polanyi, and Thomas Kuhn. See Duhem, *The Aim and Structure of Physical Theory* (New York: Atheneum, 1981); Hanson, *Patterns of Discovery* (Cambridge: Cambridge University Press, 1958); Polanyi, *Personal Knowledge: Towards a Post-Critical Philosophy* (Chicago: University of Chicago Press, 1962); and Kuhn, *The Structure of Scientific Revolutions* (Chicago: University of Chicago Press, 1970). See further A. G. Padgett, *Science and the Study of God: A Mutuality Model for Theology and Science* (Grand Rapids: Eerdmans, 2003), where I elaborate upon this basic idea and its importance for the dialogue between theology and science.

Jesus (Eph. 4:21), can and will adopt different methods for its purposes in Bible study. So my proposal for a threefold sense of Scripture is explicitly Christian. Other groups are of course free to read the Bible as they see fit, given their interests.

Beyond the Literal Sense of Scripture?

Precisely because it is a spiritual fellowship that seeks the love of God and neighbor, the church will be interested in what we might call a "spiritual" reading of the Scriptures. Yet many evangelical theologians, going back to Martin Luther himself, are skeptical of any kind of allegorical exegesis. They will insist upon the historical, literal, or plain reading of the text as alone authoritative for the church today. This is in fact an overreaction to excesses from the past, which can lead to a kind of narrow literalism that destroys the truth of Scripture. Not every part of the Bible is literally true, just because there is far too much metaphor, poetry, symbolism, and parable in the Scriptures. Those who read the Bible with open eyes can see that literal language is not the only kind of language in Scripture. At the same time, preachers excessively allegorized Scripture in the Middle Ages. Such overly allegorical readings allowed preachers to read the text in just about any way they liked. Finding the right road between these two ditches—between a narrow literalism and an excess of allegory—is what we are seeking to do here and now.

For as long as Christian theology has existed, the church has insisted upon some kind of spiritual meaning of the biblical text that goes beyond the literal or historical meaning. Even those faithful theologians who complained against the excesses of allegory, such as Diodore of Tarsus and Martin Luther, used a "fuller sense" or spiritual interpretation of the text. While I may not go as far as David Steinmetz, who argued for the superiority of precritical exegesis, I would argue that there are serious limitations to the modern and "scientific" historical-critical method that universities now teach as the right academic approach to Bible study. Equally problematic is the simple literalism of evangelicals in the eighteenth and early nineteenth centuries.[40] How shall we move beyond this impasse? In his wonderful historical overview of the allegorical interpretation of Scripture, Henri de Lubac also provides a kind of apologia for the continuation of a spiritual sense today.[41] Surely he is right about this need. But what shape shall such a spiritual reading take? How can we honor the critical insights of historical methods and the plain, original sense of the text, while at the same time doing justice to the spiritual and theological aims of the church?

I am not suggesting here a return to the allegories of the past. The main problem with the allegorical methods of old is the lack of control. Basil the Great complained that those who engage in allegorical excess "believe themselves wiser than the Holy Spirit, and bring forth their own ideas under a pretext of exegesis."[42] It was the excesses of allegory and the need for some kind of limit to imagination in textual interpretation that gave the spiritual sense of Scripture a bad name. Even though modern scholars continue to steer clear of allegory, I believe that the gospel itself demands a fuller sense of Scripture beyond the conventional meaning of the text—that is, beyond the original intent of the inspired author and/or editors. At the same time, we will still need some kind of control or limit to our theological interpretation in order to avoid eisegesis (reading meaning into a text). Finding a way between these two problems is a pressing need today.

Thus far, our argument is that a gospel-centered biblical interpretation and application may well begin with the conventional

40. D. C. Steinmetz, "The Superiority of Pre-Critical Exegesis," *ThTo* 37 (1980): 27–38; reprinted in Donald McKim, ed., *A Guide to Contemporary Hermeneutics: Major Trends in Biblical Interpretation* (Grand Rapids: Eerdmans, 1986).

41. Henri de Lubac, *Medieval Exegesis*, trans. M. Sebanc and E. M. Macierowski, 4 vols. (Grand Rapids: Eerdmans, 1998–2010). See, e.g., 1:234–41.

42. Basil of Caesarea, "Hexaemeron," hom. 9 (*NPNF*² 8:102). I owe this reference to Christopher Hall.

sense, but that it will also involve a larger, canonical sense. The unity of the books of the Bible in one canon is already a faith statement grounded in the gospel of Jesus Christ. As evangelical theologian T. F. Torrance remarks, for example, "Since the Scriptures are the result of the inspiration of the Holy Spirit by the will of the Father through Jesus Christ, and since the Word of God who speaks through all the Scriptures became incarnate in Jesus Christ, it is Jesus Christ himself who must constitute the controlling centre in all right interpretation of the Scriptures."[43] By "right interpretation," Torrance must mean a right *Christian* reading of the Bible as the Word of God, since other groups will promote their own "right" understanding of the text. Still, we can agree with Torrance, who (following his teacher Karl Barth) holds that the canonical sense is christocentric. Jesus as the living Word constitutes the controlling center of any properly Christian biblical interpretation.

Christ-Centered Bible Study

The argument against man-centered leadership that is at the heart of this book will be based on a canonical sense of Scripture, which interprets the conventional sense as we apply the Bible's message to our contemporary world. In his outstanding study of New Testament ethics, Richard Hays notes that many scholars find the canon to be irreducibly complex. He then rightly goes on to write: "The task of discerning some coherence in the canon is both necessary and possible."[44] I agree with Hays that no one theme or concept (e.g., love, covenant, justification) does justice to the complexity of the canon.[45] Instead of one or more specific themes, *the person of Jesus* provides a unity-

43. T. F. Torrance, *The Trinitarian Faith: The Evangelical Theology of the Ancient Catholic Faith* (Edinburgh: T&T Clark, 1988), 39.

44. Richard B. Hays, *The Moral Vision of the New Testament: A Contemporary Introduction to New Testament Ethics* (San Francisco: HarperSanFrancisco, 1996), 4.

45. Ibid., 5. He himself proposes community, cross, and new creation as a trio of themes that can give a holistic moral vision of the New Testament.

in-complexity for the Christian Bible. This unity includes all
that Jesus is and does—past, present, and future. My argument
is that for evangelical thought—indeed, for classic Christian
thought—the canonical sense must be christocentric.

But what about the Triune God? Is this God not the true
subject of the Christian Bible? Is a christocentric reading not
overly Western? I have argued elsewhere, in dialogue with Orthodox thought, that a christocentric reading of the whole Bible
will lead to a trinitarian God.[46] A Christ-centered approach to
Scripture does not mean that we find Jesus in every verse of the
Bible or that there is nothing more to the canonical sense than
Christ. Christ is the key to or center of this level of meaning for
the biblical text, but not the entire content. This way of reading
does not mean we engage in allegory, unless we think the text
itself is an allegory (which is rare in Scripture). If the Bible in one
verse tells us to hate our enemies, I am not suggesting that we
allegorize the word *enemy* into meaning "our sins" and so forth.
Let the text speak for itself. However, each particular text will
only be authoritative for the church today in conversation with
the larger canon. In other words, the contemporary sense works
in concert with the canonical sense and not with the conventional sense alone. My proposal for a canonical sense concerns
not allegory, but the larger significance of entire passages seen
within books and Testaments. The whole canon, then, provides
a larger context of meaning that will shape, adjust, and even
correct a particular text. Only in this way should a particular
text be authoritative for the worshiping community of faith.

So far we have found that a plain or conventional reading of
the Bible is, by itself, insufficient. In keeping with classic Christianity, we should look for a spiritual sense that goes beyond the
plain text of Scripture. These are not "steps" in interpretation
so much as layers of meaning. As a worshiping community,

46. A. G. Padgett, "The Canonical Sense of Scripture: Christocentric or Trinitarian?" *Di* 45 (2006): 36–43.

which is thus also a theological community, we will need all these layers, all the time. The second layer or sense has been the focus of this short section, but the larger argument of this book ignores neither history (conventional sense) nor application (contemporary sense). In between these two layers, at the canonical level, we find a hermeneutical principle that orients our reading of Scripture toward Jesus Christ and our life with the Triune God. These arguments lead to the following practical conclusion: a portion of the Bible is authoritative for today only when particular texts pass through the Christ-centered, canonical layer of meaning.

We will draw upon this point fully when we get to the application and results of our study later in the book. Yet perhaps even at this early stage, a short example would be helpful in pointing out the importance of reading Scripture as a whole, with Christ at the center. For centuries the church has seen the divine Trinity at work in the creation narrative of Genesis 1. After all, YHWH speaks a powerful Word of creation, and the Spirit of God is also present (Gen. 1:2). On the sixth day, God says let "us" create human beings in "our" image and likeness, using the plural (Gen. 1:26). These details have led Christian interpreters to find the Trinity in this chapter. Yet a modern critical investigation of the original context—that is to say, the conventional sense—rightly concludes that no such doctrine could possibly have been in the mind of the original author, editor, or first Hebrew readers. However, when we read this chapter in light of the New Testament, say, side by side with John 1, we can conclude that God the Son was indeed already with God the Father and the Holy Spirit from the first moment of creation. From eternity, God has always been Triune. When we read Genesis 1 in light of the whole Christian Bible, a larger Christ-centered, and so trinitarian, layer of meaning *is* legitimate—as long as we don't confuse this meaning with the original author's intention. Later chapters of this book draw on my proposal for a threefold sense of Scripture, speaking especially to the issue of submission in Scripture and for Christian discipleship today.

A Few Modest Conclusions

We have argued that evangelicals base their theology and discipleship appropriately on Jesus Christ and the gospel. The best textual evidence for Christ and the good news comes from Scripture, which we confess to be the Word of God written by human hands. Evangelical biblical ethics, therefore, will only accept the authoritative reading of the *whole* Bible on a topic, with Christ himself as the interpretive key to Scripture. No single verse in isolation is authoritative Holy Scripture on its own; only the whole Bible is the Word of God in written form, not a particular sentence or paragraph. The practical result of this theological point is that no single verse can determine what the church should think about the role relationship between men and women. We need to examine the Bible as a whole on this topic and let Christ lead us to the truth of the Scriptures.

2

Mutual Submission
and Christian Leadership

The Bible and the Ethics of Roles

What does it mean to talk about "roles" in Christian ethics? What is mutual submission, understood as a biblical ethic? Is it different from servant leadership? Those who hold to man-centered and hierarchal gender roles often insist that wives should submit to their husbands in all things. Husbands themselves do not submit to wives; they show "servant leadership" instead.[1] The purpose of this chapter is to call this distinction into question by taking a fresh look at the issue of leadership in the New Testament. In keeping with an evangelical approach, we will look to Christ and hold him at the center of our understanding of leadership and submission for biblical ethics. As we will see, not only is Jesus the key example

1. See among many examples the contribution of George W. Knight III to John Piper and Wayne Grudem, eds., *Recovering Biblical Manhood and Womanhood*, 2nd ed. (Wheaton: Crossway, 2006), chaps. 8 and 20 of the new edition.

of mutual submission for the New Testament, he is also the key example of servant leadership. The twentieth-century term *servant leadership*, we will discover, describes but one way of living in mutual submission. While mutual submission and servant leadership are not *identical*, servant leadership is one way of talking about the *form* that mutual submission takes when one is a leader. Before showing from Scripture what Christian leadership is like, we need to take a quick look at the notion of "roles" in the human story.

Narrative and the Ethics of Roles

As we noted in the previous chapter, the new revisionist theory we now call complementarian made central the notion of roles in a biblical ethic of man and woman. Women in this new perspective are now seen (thank God!) as equal to men. Like men, they are fully human and fully in the image of God. But what this position gives with the one hand, it takes with the other. While women are said to be equal in being, for complementarians their *roles* are now different. The roles of men and women are supposed to complement each other and thus maintain the important *differences* between them. The view we call mutual submission certainly agrees that the differing roles of women and men in society and family do indeed complement each other. The real problem with complementarian views is their man-centered notion of authority. While the role of women may well include some areas of leadership, Christian women should continue to submit to the authority of some man: husband, father, and/or male senior pastor. Of course, men too will submit to proper authority; but the key problem is the gendered character of that authority in complementarian views. In the family, wives and daughters must submit to the "spiritual headship" of the man (husband or father). In the church, women may indeed have some religious authority, but they must be under the "spiritual headship" of the male senior pastor.[2]

It is clear, therefore, that the ethics of this revisionist view is based on the notion of gender roles for men and women. What has not been carefully discussed in the literature overall is the very idea of an ethic based on roles. What is the nature of a role, and what is its meaning from an ethical standpoint? In what way do roles play a part of our interrelational, complex moral life?

The existence of books on professional ethics requires us to think about this question: What kind of roles are gender roles, morally?[3] Are they something intrinsic, something proper to the persons themselves, or do their moral aspects apply *only* to the role? For example, when a person takes up the role of a physician, she takes up a number of moral duties, such as the obligation to maintain the confidentiality of her conversations with patients. This moral duty does not apply only to the role; the doctor herself is involved in her own moral integrity. The same goes for the role of pastor and the confidential character of many pastoral conversations. On the other hand, some professional roles, such as that of a criminal defense attorney, have moral aspects that apply only to the role itself; they do not attach to the person outside of this role. The role of the attorney is to present the very best case for the defendant he can. The prosecution, judge, and jury also have roles to play, each related to the court and the legal process. To play his role properly and morally in our system of justice, a lawyer may be called upon to defend in court an action that he might otherwise condemn

2. As mentioned in the previous chapter, the most influential work advocating complementarian views is Piper and Grudem, *Recovering Biblical Manhood and Womanhood*.

3. For example, Arthur I. Applbaum, *Ethics for Adversaries: The Morality of Roles in Public and Professional Life* (Princeton: Princeton University Press, 1999), or Justin Oakley, *Virtue Ethics and Professional Roles* (Cambridge: Cambridge University Press, 2001). See also the earlier works by two philosophers, R. S. Downie, *Roles and Values* (London: Methuen, 1971); and Dorothy Emmet, *Rules, Roles and Relation* (London: Macmillan, 1966).

outside of this legal context. In this case, the morality of the role does not apply properly to the person.

In this work we will place the ethics of roles in the broader context of Christian discipleship and mutual submission based on biblical ethics. The roles we play as disciples of Christ are various, and the way in which we fulfill Jesus' ethic of love will depend upon the context. From the outset, it needs to be clear that *the ethic of mutual submission is best understood as a voluntary taking up of the role of a servant or slave in relation to one another*. But the virtues and character that are displayed in these acts of love are proper to the believer. The roles may come and go, but loving actions are real displays of the underlying character of the disciple, which itself is modeled on Christ. We should use the word *character*, therefore, for a stable set of moral dispositions—that is, habits that will be good or bad, virtues or vices.[4] A biblical example of this point is made in 1 Peter 5:5: "In the same way, you young ones, be subject to the elders [or possibly "to the older members"]. All of you should clothe yourselves with humility toward one another, for 'God opposes the proud but gives grace to the humble.'"

The underlying character trait enjoined in this example from Scripture is that of humility. Humility is part of a good Christian character, and that virtue can be part of who we are as disciples in many times and contexts. According to this text, both elders and young people should act with humility toward each other. In the case of the young, being humble means submitting to their elders. But people are not always young. Still, even when they grow up, believers should be humble in the way they treat

---

4. This notion of a moral character that is stable over time goes back to Aristotle (*Nicomachean Ethics* 2.1), but was adopted by many other philosophers over the centuries. For a contemporary example, see Paul Ricoeur, *Oneself as Another* (Chicago: University of Chicago Press, 1992), 120: "Character . . . designates the set of lasting dispositions by which a person is recognized." In this section Ricoeur rightly notes that this understanding of character necessarily implies persons exist over time. Character ethics is connected to temporality.

one another. So here we see an example of a character trait or virtue that remains over time, while the particular situation (and thus the role played) is bound to change. The role we play as young person or elder in the church will change, but the virtue of humility is constant and reflects the character of the believer.

What holds for the nature of character and roles in this example should also hold for the gender roles we play in our complex social lives. These roles are also means of showing our moral character, our virtues or our vices. A mother who feeds her children or a father who helps his children get dressed for school is not *just* acting out a role; they each bring their own moral character to bear in the way they fulfill their roles. It would seem, then, that the morality of our gender roles *is* proper to our person. A moral failing in the way one fulfills a gender role (e.g., when parents need to discipline their child or when spouses need to discuss a divisive issue) is therefore a moral failing for that person *per se*. If I am violent and cruel in the way I fulfill my gender role, that is a moral failing for me as a person. My moral failure implies that my character is a "vicious" one (that is, one with vices). A lack of morality in this instance does not apply only to my role as husband or father. In the same way, if one is an exemplary mother, father, husband, or wife, that is a moral achievement for a person. One's morality in this instance does not simply apply to the role itself.

To summarize our point thus far: some roles that humans fill in society do not clearly display a person's moral character, at least not as a rule. A good construction worker or a good computer technician may or may not be a *morally* good person. As long as they do their job correctly, they have fulfilled their obligations. But gender roles do reflect a person's moral character. A good mother or father, a good wife or husband, is to some degree a good *person*. We might call these "morally direct" roles, while the other kinds of roles are morally indirect or ambiguous.

We have concluded that the morally direct roles we play, such as those involving being a disciple or in our gender relationships, are not merely external to our character. They are part of the way we display and develop our moral character *per se*, part of who we are as a person. We are talking here about an ethic of character instead of an ethic of rules or laws. Unlike an ethic of rules or laws, an ethic of character (and of roles) requires *time*. We live out and develop our character over time and in the midst of a community. We might say, then, that an ethic of character and an ethic of roles take place *within a human narrative*. For this reason, Christian scholars who work on the ethics of character also work on *narrative* ethics.[5]

Narratives, whether historical or fictional, do require more than time, community, and characters. There are many theories of narrative that, while interesting, are best saved for another time and place.[6] Yet the topic we are considering, the ethics of roles, requires that we make some rudimentary points. To take up a role requires a *person* who plays that role. This role takes place in a complex social situation, with a wide variety of interpersonal elements at play. In other words, living out a morally direct role requires some kind of human *community*. This social situation will include issues of space and social structure, but it will also include *history*. Playing a role takes time, evolves over time, and involves our relationships with other people and with larger social contexts. A narrative, however,

5. My thinking on this topic has been particularly influenced by Alasdair MacIntyre, Paul Ricoeur, and Stanley Hauerwas. See MacIntyre, *After Virtue*, 2nd ed. (Notre Dame, IN: University of Notre Dame Press, 1984), and *Three Rival Versions of Moral Enquiry* (Notre Dame, IN: University of Notre Dame Press, 1990); Ricoeur, *Time and Narrative*, 3 vols. (Chicago: University of Chicago Press, 1984–88), and *Oneself as Another*; Hauerwas, *A Community of Character* (Notre Dame, IN: University of Notre Dame Press, 1981); and Hauerwas and L. G. Jones, eds., *Why Narrative?* (Grand Rapids: Eerdmans, 1989).

6. For one introduction among several, see James Phelen and P. J. Rabinowitz, eds., *A Companion to Narrative Theory* (Oxford: Blackwell, 2005).

requires even more elements, including a plot and some kind of coherent story, whether historical or literary (fictional). For our purposes, we can stop our analysis with these three elements: character, community, and time.

The Bible contains an ethic of character, an ethic of virtues and vices. Of course, it also has many commandments and rules, most notably the Ten Commandments. But rules are not all there is in biblical ethics. For Christians the most important story of a virtuous life is found in the Gospels. The teachings and example of Jesus provide Christianity with a powerful narrative ethic of character. Our purpose in this book is to apply the model of Christ to the ethics of gender roles. Having outlined some considerations regarding the ethics of roles, we now turn to the Scriptures to examine the notion of submission and also to show that Jesus took up the role of a servant toward his disciples, and indeed toward humanity as a whole.

The Bible and the Ethics of Submission

Submission is not a positive word in American culture or ethical thinking. This is particularly true among those who work for justice for the poor, the oppressed, and the marginalized.[7] But the biblical ethic of submission is not what we tend to think it is. The evangelical thinker who is biblically based must work hard to understand and live out the Bible's ethic of submission in a way that does not imply further violence toward the oppressed. Here we will take a careful look at what the Bible says about submission and discipleship. Later in this chapter we will show that Jesus provides us with a moral example of freely taking up the role of a servant—that is, of a certain type of submission.

7. For a helpful consideration of the ethics of submission and power by a contemporary feminist theologian, see Sarah Coakley, *Powers and Submissions* (Oxford: Blackwell, 2002).

On Submission

The Greek words for submission in the Bible are usually either *hypotagē* or *hypotassō*.[8] While the idea of submission occurs in several places in the New Testament without the use of one of these two (Greek) words, we will start our investigation with a word study. Our particular interest is in the verb, *hypotassō*, because of its larger range of meaning, and also because it is the verb used in Ephesians 5:21.

The Greek word *hypotassō* has a larger range of meanings than "to submit" in English.[9] It can mean any kind of ordering under something or someone. Thus it may mean to put something after or under another thing, or even to add something to the end of a document. For example, in the Apostolic Fathers, Polycarp writes that the letters of Ignatius "are appended [*hypotetagmenai*] to this letter."[10] Polycarp's usage indicates clearly a much broader meaning than *submit* has in English. Yet in many contexts, including military and political ones, *submission* means just what we might normally think—namely, an involuntary obedience to an external authority. This kind of submission requires obedience and, while it may be done with a good attitude and a desire to obey, it also requires compliance. In this study we will call this *type I submission*. For example, the Greek Old Testament (Septuagint [or LXX]) uses the verb *hypotassō* to speak of "the tribute of those that *were subject*" to King Solomon (1 Kings 10:15).

The burden of this section of the book is to show that this is not the only sense of the verb. P. T. O'Brien correctly gives the general sense of this verb as "to arrange under."[11] Especially

8. See G. Delling, "*hypotassō, hypotagē*," *TDNT* 8:39–47; "*hypotassō*" and "*hypotagē*," BDAG 1041–42.

9. See "*hypotassō*," in H. G. Liddell, et al., *A Greek-English Lexicon*, 9th ed. (Oxford: Oxford University Press, 1983), 1897.

10. Polycarp, *To the Philippians* 13.1, in J. B. Lightfoot, M. R. Harmer, and M. W. Holmes, eds., *The Apostolic Fathers*, 2nd ed. (Grand Rapids: Baker Books, 1992), 218.

11. P. T. O'Brien, *The Letter to the Ephesians*, PNTC (Grand Rapids: Eerdmans, 1999), 399. We will take up O'Brien's arguments against mutual submission when we exegete this passage more fully.

when used with the middle voice (which in Greek means that one does the action to or for oneself), the verb *hypotassō* can take on the sense of a voluntary submission to another person out of humility, compassion, or love.[12] This we will call *type II submission*.

Hypotassō has a wide range of meanings. Complementarian scholars often narrowly restrict the meaning of this Greek verb in the middle voice to involuntary submission to a recognized authority. It would likewise be inaccurate to claim that mutual submission means something as weak as "acting in love" or "being thoughtful to each other"; rather, the term *submission* implies something more self-sacrificial. Mutual submission in practice is taking up the role of a slave toward one another. So it is too rigid a reading of the verb to insist, as Piper and Grudem do, that "the term always implies a relationship of submission to an authority."[13] Egalitarian scholars can sometimes make the same mistake. In his important book advocating mutual submission between women and men, Gilbert Bilezikian claims that "'submit' means to make oneself subordinate to the authority of a higher power . . . to yield to rulership."[14] Despite my respect

12. On the middle voice, see H. W. Smyth, *Greek Grammar* (Cambridge, MA: Harvard University Press, 1920), §§1713–21. An early but sometimes neglected argument for this second sense of submission is Else Kähler, "Zur Unterordnung der Frau im Neuen Testament," *ZEE* 3 (1959): 1–13; see also her larger study, *Die Frau in den paulinischen Briefen* (Zürich: Goffthelf, 1960). See also Delling, "*hypotassō*," *TDNT* 8:41–45; M. Barth, *Ephesians 4–6*, AB 34A (New York: Doubleday, 1974), 608–11, 700–715; John H. Yoder, *The Politics of Jesus*, 2nd ed. (Grand Rapids: Eerdmans, 1994), chap. 9; Gilbert Bilezikian, *Beyond Sex Roles*, 3rd ed. (Grand Rapids: Baker Academic, 2006), chap. 5; and Alan Johnson, "A Christian Understanding of Submission," *PriscPap* 17, no. 4 (Fall 2003): 11–20.

13. Piper and Grudem, *Recovering Biblical Manhood and Womanhood* (1991 ed.), 493n. For a similarly narrow misreading of the verb in its middle voice, see Wayne Grudem, *Evangelical Feminism and Biblical Truth* (Sisters, OR: Multnomah, 2004), 188–200. Both texts impose a quite rigid interpretation on the lexical evidence. On the contrary, as G. Delling rightly cautions us, "For a material understanding of the verb in the NT its considerable range of meaning should be noted, especially in the middle" ("*hypotassō*," *TDNT* 8:41).

14. Bilezikian, *Beyond Sex Roles*, 117.

for these biblical scholars, such one-sided interpretations do not fit the larger lexical evidence.

Let us consider just one example from the Greek Bible. In 162 BC, the emperor Antiochus V and his army invaded Judea and were met by the army of Judas Maccabeus. Because the imperial regent Philip was in open rebellion in another locale, the emperor and his army were forced to sue for peace with the Jews. Second Maccabees puts the point this way: Antiochus "*yielded (hypetagē)* and swore to observe all their rights, made peace with them and offered sacrifice" (13:23).[15] That an emperor like Antiochus V, son of the notorious tyrant Antiochus IV Epiphanes, would think of this act as a submission to the "higher power" of Judas, or yielding to his "rulership" or higher authority, is historically beyond belief.[16] Even the author of Second Maccabees, Judeocentric as he was, is not suggesting this much in the text. The point is simply that Antiochus yielded to their demands. He yielded in the sense of giving up his war against them and submitting to their demands so as to make peace. We have to conclude from usage outside the New Testament that an authoritarian structure behind this verb is present sometimes but not universally.

Mutual Submission in the Pauline Epistles

There are several passages in the Epistles in which a sense of voluntary submission out of care for the other is quite clear. Type II submission is a central ethical teaching in the New Testament, and it is typically mutual—that is, it applies to every member of the body of Christ. In the next section we will look at the submission of Christ himself as the key example of type II

15. For a general discussion of the passage, see Jonathan Goldstein, *II Maccabees*, AB (New York: Doubleday, 1983), 467.

16. See the articles on Antiochus IV and V by B. K. Waltke in G. Bromiley et al., eds., *International Standard Bible Encyclopedia*, rev. ed. (Grand Rapids: Eerdmans, 1979–88), 1:145–46.

submission in the New Testament. First, though, we will examine passages in the Epistles concerning mutual submission
within the church.

The best-known example comes from Ephesians 5:21. After
giving two other commandments in Ephesians 5 concerning the
Christian way of life in the world—"Be careful how you walk,
not as unwise but as wise" (5:15) and "Do not get drunk with
wine but be filled with the Spirit" (5:18)—Paul transitions to the
theme of wives and husbands with this command: "Submit[ting]
yourselves one to another in reverence for ["fear of"] Christ."[17]
While at least one scholar has argued that the command to
submit to one another means only that the inferior member
should submit to the superior, this interpretation does not do
justice to the text or its larger context.[18] The term *one another*
(*allēlois*) in Ephesians (4:2, 32) and in Paul's letters in general
indicates something that applies to each member of the church
and not merely to a few.[19] Just as the other commands in Ephesians 5:15–20 apply to all Christians, so does this one—a point
we will press later in our interpretation of the whole passage.
Our initial point here is a simple one: voluntary self-submission
is a general principle for all Christians, not just women or slaves.
The concrete nature of this submission is indicated at the end
of this passage, in which Paul returns to this theme: "However,
each of you [husbands] should love his wife as himself, and the
wife should revere ["fear," as in 5:21] her husband" (5:33).

Here Paul insists that, in their roles as husband and wife,
Christians in Ephesus should exemplify mutual submission by
the husband's self-sacrificial love and voluntary self-submission,

17. In this work I will use the name Paul to speak of the author of any of the letters that open with the apostle's name. This is a matter of convenience; we cannot
here enter into the significant debate concerning Pauline authorship of Ephesians and
other disputed Pauline letters.

18. S. B. Clark, *Man and Woman in Christ* (Ann Arbor, MI: Servant, 1980), 74;
see the critical response in E. Best, *Ephesians*, ICC (Edinburgh: T&T Clark, 1998),
516. We will pursue this point more fully when we consider the passage as a whole.

19. See Romans 1:12; 15:5; Galatians 5:13, 17, 26.

with the wife returning the same. We can now show from other Pauline texts that the command to submit to one another, understood as taking up the role of a slave or servant, applies to all Christians, of every worldly rank. The point is very much in keeping with the other "one another" passages in Ephesians: "Lead a life worthy of the calling to which you have been called, with all humility and gentleness, with patience, bearing with one another in love" (4:1b–2 NRSV); "Be kind to one another, tenderhearted, forgiving one another, as God in Christ forgave you" (4:32).

An excellent example of mutual submission is also found in 1 Corinthians 7. It is just as clear a case of mutual submission as in Ephesians 5, but is not as well known. Indeed, most Christian men in North America will know a little bit about "wives submitting" in Ephesians 5 but have probably never heard or read a discussion of 1 Corinthians 7 in terms of mutual submission. To understand rightly what Paul is up to in this text, we have to place it in context. Paul is writing to correct errors and problems at Corinth, some of which he learned about through their letter to him and others through his wide network of co-workers in the gospel (1 Cor. 1:11; 7:1). In several chapters of 1 Corinthians, including 6, 7, 8, and 11, Paul makes reference to, describes, and sometimes even quotes directly from what he knows of the viewpoint some Corinthian Christians held. If one of these references is widely understood to be from the Corinthian letter to Paul, more recent translations will put the phrase in quotation marks. An example of this is 1 Corinthians 7:1: "It is well for a man not to touch a woman" (NRSV).

It is generally accepted that Paul's opponents at Corinth were very ascetic, that is, their spirituality was "world-denying" and tended to see having sexual relationships as less spiritual than remaining celibate. Although Paul himself was celibate, he does not condone the Corinthian view quoted in 7:1. Rather, he specifically tells husbands and wives not to neglect their sexual relationship "except perhaps by mutual consent [*ek symphōnou*] for a season" (7:5). Note the emphasis on *mutual* consent, not the authority of the husband. Just prior to this verse, Paul makes a statement that is radically egalitarian for its day in the way he talks about the mutual "rights" of husband and wife: "Let the husband give to his wife what is owed her, and likewise the wife to the husband. For the wife does not have authority over her own body, but the husband does. Likewise the husband does not have authority over his own body, but the wife does" (7:3–4).[20] In the context of patriarchal Jewish, Greek, and Roman views about the rights of the husband in marriage, this text stands out as particularly egalitarian. Note the tone of mutual submission here, expressed in terms of the authority or power (*exousia*) that the spouse has over the person/body of his or her partner. This passage stands in stark contrast to the complementarian claim that in the New Testament husbands are given authority ("headship") over their wives. The comment by Piper and Grudem that this text merely gives "shape" to the leadership of the husband is another example of how complementarian authors can impose their views on the text.[21] Paul is here giving leadership to the wife, not "shaping" the leadership of the husband!

The idea of mutual submission between all Christians (not just wives and husbands) is expressed again in Galatians. Paul writes, "For freedom Christ has set you free" (5:1). But this is

20. The translation of 7:3–4 is from Hays, *Moral Vision*. On the egalitarian character of this passage, see Hays, *Moral Vision*, 47–51, who rightly interprets this as mutual submission (49). See further my earlier debate with Elisabeth Schüssler Fiorenza over this and other texts in 1 Corinthians: A. G. Padgett, "Feminism in First Corinthians: A Dialogue with Elisabeth Schüssler Fiorenza," *EvQ* 58 (1986): 121–32, esp. 126, where I draw upon the influential article by Robin Scroggs, "Paul and the Eschatological Woman," *JAAR* 40 (1972): 283–303, and the work of my former teacher, Darrell J. Doughty, "Heiligkeit und Freiheit" (PhD diss., University of Göttingen, 1965). Doughty's dissertation influenced to some degree the commentary by H. Conzelmann, *1 Corinthians*, Hermeneia (Philadelphia: Fortress, 1975), see esp. 114–17.

21. Piper and Grudem, *Recovering Biblical Manhood and Womanhood* (1991 ed.), 88. Despite the fact that Paul deals at length with marriage in 1 Corinthians 7, there is no section in this large anthology devoted to 1 Corinthians 7.

not a freedom to do whatever we want. He goes on in 5:13 to say, "Do not use your freedom as an opportunity for the flesh, but through love be slaves to one another [*douleuete allēlois*]." The Greek verb *douleuō* comes from the word for slave (*doulos*) and means "to be a slave," "to act like a slave," or "to serve."[22] Paul does not mean that each member of the church should actually *be* a slave. Rather, his command means that we should act like a slave or take up the role of a slave out of love for one another. But what does it mean to act like a slave in Paul's world? In a careful study of slavery in the Greco-Roman world and as a metaphor in Paul's writings, Dale Martin notes that "slavery can operate as a metaphor in this way because a slave's activities were also supposedly pursued with a view to the interests of the owner and with no prospect of self-interest. In fact, slavery was commonly defined as living for the benefit or profit of another."[23] To take up the role of a slave, then, is to act not for self-interest but to serve the other person with his or her best interests firmly in mind. This notion of taking up the role of a slave in love toward one another provides us with a much more concrete image of the general Christian command to love one another. Paul applies this idea in 2 Corinthians when he says of himself, "We preach not ourselves, but Jesus Christ as lord, and ourselves as your slaves for the sake of Jesus" (4:5).

To take up the role of a slave toward one another in love is very much in keeping with the ethics of the New Testament in general and with what Paul has to say to the church generally. For example, in Romans 15:1–3 Paul uses different words to say very much the same thing that he said in Galatians 5:13, this time connecting these ideals to the model of Christ (as in Eph. 5): "We who are strong ought to bear with the failings of

22. See "*douleuō*," BDAG 260. On this passage and the letter as a whole, see the fine study by John Barclay, *Obeying the Truth: Paul's Ethics in Galatians* (Minneapolis: Fortress, 1991).

23. Dale Martin, *Slavery as Salvation: The Metaphor of Slavery in Pauline Christianity* (New Haven: Yale University Press, 1990), 50–51.

the weak, and not please [*areskein*] ourselves. Let each of us please our neighbor, for his or her own good, to build them up; for Christ did not please himself." The behavior Paul exhorts here is very similar to the role of a slave as explained by Martin: working for the benefit of the owner rather than for self-interest. It finds a clear echo in 1 Corinthians 10:24: "Let no one seek their own good, but the good of the other." The model of taking up the role of a slave as a form of gospel-centered leadership also illuminates some of the things Paul says about his ministry. For example, in 1 Corinthians 10:33 he states, "I try to please [*areskō*] all people in everything, not seeking my own advantage but that of the many, so that they may be saved." Paul takes up the role of a slave to "the many" out of love for them and for the gospel of salvation, in keeping with his apostleship and calling to be a "slave of Christ" (Rom. 1:1; Phil. 1:1).

Taken together, Romans, 1–2 Corinthians, and Galatians are central to Pauline thought and can help us better understand the command in Ephesians to submit to one another out of reverence for Christ. This way of reading is in keeping with an evangelical biblical theology in which the larger, canonical sense of a text within the whole of Scripture, with Christ as the centerpoint of interpretation, is the lens by which we interpret the written Word for today. A very clear instance in which the submission of Jesus is a moral example for mutual submission in the church comes from Philippians.

Philippians may be best known for its beautiful hymnlike homage to Christ in 2:6–11. Whatever its origins before its inclusion here (and there are many theories and works devoted to this question), the text is now an integral part of the letter.[24] Paul points to Christ as an ethical example both for himself and

---

24. For one monograph among many devoted to Philippians 2:6–11, see Ralph P. Martin, *A Hymn of Christ* (Downers Grove, IL: InterVarsity, 1997); earlier editions were published under the title *Carmen Christi*. This work reviews various theories and has a significant bibliography.

for the church with special reference to what this text says about
him. The chapter in which this famous passage occurs begins
this way: "If there is any comfort in Christ, any motivation from
love, any communion [*koinōnia*] in the Spirit, any friendship
or sympathy, fill up my joy by being of one accord [*to auto
phronēte*], having the same love, united mind [*hen phronountes*]
and soul. Do nothing from selfishness or arrogance, but in humility count others as more important than yourself. Let each
of you look after not only your own interest but the interests
of others. Have this mind [*phroneite*] among yourselves, which
was also in Christ Jesus" (Phil. 2:1–5). In this opening section
of chapter 2, Paul exhorts his listeners, as he does elsewhere, to
take up the role of a slave and, out of love, to act not for their
own self-interest but for the interest of the other. As Sydney
Park has shown in a recent monograph, without using the word
submission Paul is speaking here about submission.[25]

Even more clearly than in Romans 15, Paul makes Jesus the
standard and moral exemplar of this kind of loving service.
Three times Paul uses a Greek word for practical, ethical wisdom: *phronēsis* (the verb form *phronein* is used ten times in Philippians). This kind of wisdom or way of thinking ("mind") was
especially important for character ethics in Greek philosophy.
Thus in the Greek text, the ethical thrust of Paul's appeal is even
more evident. Jesus is being set up as one whose moral way of
thinking the church is supposed to imitate. In this way the church
can "live as citizens in a manner worthy of the gospel of Christ"

25. M. Sydney Park, *Submission within the Godhead and the Church in the Epistle
to the Philippians* (London: T&T Clark, 2007). I have found the work of Stephen Fowl
on this text to be particularly instructive. See S. E. Fowl, "Christology and Ethics in
Philippians 2:5–11," in *Where Christology Began: Essays on Philippians 2*, ed. R. P.
Martin and B. J. Dodd (Louisville: Westminster John Knox, 1998), 140–53; and his
earlier monograph *The Story of Christ in the Ethics of Paul*, JSNTSup (Sheffield: Shef-
field Academic Press, 1990). Both Fowl and N. T. Wright (*The Climax of the Covenant*
[Edinburgh: T&T Clark, 1991]) develop themes from the influential article by C. F. D.
Moule, "Further Reflections on Philippians 2:5–11," in *Apostolic History and the
Gospel*, ed. Ralph Martin and Ward Gasque (Grand Rapids: Eerdmans, 1970), 264–76.

(Phil. 1:27). Since the issue is one of character ethics and taking up a role, it is not simply one of *imitation*. The Christian is not to imitate the heavenly descent and ascent of Christ portrayed in 2:6–11. The point is not to ask, what would Jesus do?, but to ask what it means to apply the character virtues and wisdom of Jesus to this particular situation. In the ethics of roles, this would mean *living out the virtues and ethical wisdom of Jesus in a particular role and context*. Stephen Fowl makes the point this way: "The story of Christ narrated in 2:6–11 functions as an exemplar, a concrete expression of a shared norm from which Paul and the Philippians can make analogical judgments about how they should live."[26] In his humiliation and service to others, Jesus had an ethical "mind" that we Christians need to learn from and exemplify.[27] His character thus becomes the standard for mutual submission, just because he took up the role of a slave out of obedience to God.

The next part of the chapter (vv. 6–11) is fraught with exegetical issues, and a great amount of literature has developed around it.[28] Here is one way to translate the text into English:

> . . . [Jesus Christ,] [6]who, being in the form of God, did not consider equality with God as something for his own advantage [*harpagmon*], [7]but made himself nothing [*ekenōsen*, "emptied himself"], taking the form of a slave, being born in the likeness of human beings [8]and appearing as a human, he humbled himself and became obedient unto death, even death on a cross. [9]Therefore God also highly exalted him and bestowed on him the name that is above every name; [10]that at the name of Jesus

---

26. Fowl, "Christology and Ethics," 145–46.

27. See Fowl, "Christology and Ethics," and Wayne A. Meeks, "The Man from Heaven in Paul's Letter to the Philippians," in *The Future of Early Christianity*, ed. B. A. Pearson (Minneapolis: Fortress, 1991).

28. For an exegetical overview of the passage, with bibliography, see G. F. Hawthorne, *Philippians*, WBC (Waco: Word, 1983), 71–96; or, more recently, Gordon Fee, *Paul's Letter to the Philippians*, NICNT (Grand Rapids: Eerdmans, 1995), 39–46, 191–229.

every knee should bow, in heaven, on earth, and under the earth,
[11]and every tongue confess that Jesus Christ is Lord to the glory
of God the Father.[29]

Most interpreters see this passage as a narrative of Christ's descent from heaven and glorious exaltation back to heavenly authority.

In this story, verse 8 is central: Christ's death on the cross is the most striking element of his self-humiliation. The "emptying" of Christ should be read here (v. 7) as a metaphor for making oneself of no regard or glory. The text knows nothing of a strong metaphysical "kenosis" developed later by patristic theologians. In taking on the form or role of a slave, Christ did not consider his equality with God something to keep hold of for his own advantage (this phrase in v. 6 is often translated "to grasp"; cf. NRSV, "as something to be exploited"). Instead, he followed the path of humble service all the way to Golgotha in obedience to God. In other words, while Christians can never imitate Christ's self-humiliation and full exaltation, the character displayed by Jesus is the fullest and best model for Christians of the kind of mutual submission—that is, taking up the role of a slave, out of love toward one another—that Paul has just been urging (Phil. 2:1–5).

From this lyrical story of Christ's humiliation and exaltation, Paul goes on to draw specific ethical applications, starting with "and so, my beloved, just as you have always obeyed" (v. 12). It is interesting to note that in discussing other church leaders in this chapter, Paul complains that many of them—in contrast to Timothy—look after their own interests rather than those of Jesus Christ (v. 21). In other words, they do not act properly as "slaves" of Christ.

In drawing to a close this discussion of mutual submission (that is, type II submission) in the Epistles, we see they enjoin

29. My reading of verse 6 in particular, and of the text as a whole, is influenced by Wright, *Climax of the Covenant*, who picks up on some themes from Moule, "Further Reflections on Philippians 2:5–11."

a mutual humility and self-giving service on everyone in the Christian body, whether they are elders or young people, male or female. In Paul we find a connection between such mutual submission and the act of taking up the role of a good slave. As understood in his context, "good" slaves looked after the owner's interest rather than their own. In Christian thought, such a model of self-giving care for another was *mutual* within the body of Christ. Although top-down submission (type I) can hardly be mutual, that is not the only kind of submission. Mutual self-giving love is another type of submission that all believers are meant to enact toward one another. This role is one that is grounded in the character and moral wisdom of Christ Jesus. To him we now turn for further elaboration of mutual submission.

Leadership as Taking the Role of a Servant

Where did the ethic of mutual submission in the Epistles come from? A very likely source historically is Jesus himself.[30] In all four Gospels, Jesus consistently teaches and lives out a model of leadership that is loving servanthood in action.[31] Since both the Gospels and the Epistles in the New Testament are the literary remains of the powerful person and teachings of Jesus, the most reasonable historical origin of the ethic of mutuality in the Epistles is Jesus. We will show exegetically in this section that "servant leadership" and taking up the role of a servant, as taught by Jesus, are essentially the same idea or practice. From this conclusion it will follow that mutual submission and

30. For a critical-exegetical study of the ethics of the historical Jesus, see W. Schrage, *The Ethics of the New Testament* (Philadelphia: Fortress, 1988), §I; and Allen Verhey, *The Great Reversal: Ethics and the New Testament* (Grand Rapids: Eerdmans, 1988), 1–60, 72–102.

31. My views on the teaching of Jesus in this regard have been shaped by the important 1972 work of John H. Yoder, *The Politics of Jesus*. I have also benefited from the study by Hays, *Moral Vision*.

servant leadership are not as distinct as hierarchic thinkers often imply. Indeed, the origin of the concept of servant leadership in recent decades makes this clear.

On Servant Leadership

The recent growth of literature in management theory and leadership studies regarding the philosophy of servant leadership can be traced back to the Quaker author, manager, and social theorist Robert K. Greenleaf (1904–90). His booklet "The Servant as Leader" (1970) created and applied the language and idea of servant leadership to organizational life.[32] His argument is that the proper kind of leader, the one that the world most needs today, is a person who puts service to others first and is not concerned to have control over or authority over others: "The servant-leader *is* servant first. . . . It begins with the natural feeling that one wants to serve, to serve *first*. . . . That person is sharply different from one who is leader first. . . . For such it will be a later choice to serve, after leadership is established."[33] His later book, *Servant Leadership* (1977), was one of the most influential works in management theory in the twentieth century. As in his earlier booklet, Greenleaf contrasts the servant leader with the boss who inhabits the top of a hierarchy, calling this arrangement the "hierarchy principle."[34] Servant leadership and seeking to control others, seeking to establish one's own authority, are diametrically opposed principles of leadership. In current leadership studies the idea of "control over" is not equated with leadership, especially since Greenleaf's work has been of some influence. Within the larger framework of servant

32. Robert K. Greenleaf, "The Servant as Leader" (1970), reprinted in Robert K. Greenleaf, *The Servant-Leader Within*, ed. Hamilton Beazley, Julie Beggs, and Larry Spears (Mahwah, NJ: Paulist Press, 2003), 29–74. The booklet was expanded and revised in Greenleaf, *Servant Leadership* (Mahwah, NJ: Paulist Press, 1977).

33. Greenleaf, *Servant Leadership*, 13 (italics in the original).

34. Ibid., 61, 85–86.

leadership, leadership has more to do with responsibility and care than with top-down control and authority.[35]

This perspective means that leadership and "authority over" are not the same thing at all, yet this assumption lies behind too much evangelical thinking that calls itself complementarian but is in fact a new form of gender hierarchy.[36] Wayne Grudem, for example, writes that "egalitarians wrongly pit servant leadership against authority"; but this remark shows little understanding of the idea of servant leadership either in the teachings of Jesus or in recent management theory.[37] The very idea of servant leadership pits itself against leadership understood as "authority over" or "ruler over." We now turn to the teachings of Jesus to demonstrate that true leadership in Christ means taking the role of a servant and not seeking a kind of leadership that is ruling over or holding authority over the other.

Leadership according to the Teachings of Jesus: Be the Servant of All

That Jesus taught his disciples to serve others rather than to lord it over them is generally accepted by students of Scripture. The evidence is too strong to think otherwise. We will demonstrate here by reference to the Gospels that, for Jesus, being a leader or "first" means being "the servant of all," that is, taking up the role of a servant (Mark 9:35). In this way we will show that the teachings of Jesus in the Gospels concerning leadership

35. See the helpful summary of the principles of servant leadership by Larry Spears in his introduction to Greenleaf, *Servant-Leader Within*, 16–19.

36. Male leadership consistently means "authority over" (sometimes called "headship" or "eldership") in Piper and Grudem, *Recovering Biblical Manhood and Womanhood* (1991 ed.), e.g., 52–54, 60–61, 64. This is why their view is rightly seen as gender hierarchy, despite their protest that their view should not be called "hierarchicalist" (xv).

37. Grudem, *Evangelical Feminism and Biblical Truth*, 168.

are practically equivalent (that is, equivalent in practice) to the mutual submission prescribed in the Epistles.[38]

The Gospel usually designated as "according to Mark" is anonymous, brief, and generally considered to be the earliest of the four Gospels. This Gospel alone contains enough material to demonstrate our point—namely, that for Jesus leadership means service, understood as taking up the role of a servant. In two places, Mark 9:33–37 and 10:41–45, Jesus specifically addresses this issue. In the first passage, Jesus asks his disciples what they were discussing or debating as they journeyed along the road to Capernaum. They do not answer him, for their debate was about "who was the greatest" (9:34). The term *greatest* here, and the rest of what Jesus has to say, suggests they were discussing who had or would have precedence and prestige among them. Questions of precedence and rank were quite common in the culture of Judea at that time.[39] Of course, such questions are common enough in most cultures, simply because humans are in many ways tribal animals. Jesus' reply to their (hidden) question is decisive: if anyone wants to be first (in rank), they must be last and the servant (or slave) of all (9:35). In other words, rank or authority among the followers of Jesus is to be decided by servanthood, not by who has the power and the glory in worldly terms. To be great or first in God's kingdom is to be a servant—in fact, the servant of all. In Matthew's version of this saying, Jesus makes this explicit: "Whoever humbles themselves like this child is the greatest in the kingdom of heaven" (18:4). We might be tempted to simply think of this as an attitude, as having "a servant's heart." But notice what Jesus says. He does not call for an attitude or emotion but for action: *be* the servant of all. Yet it is also true

38. The basic point is also made in Yoder, *Politics of Jesus*; Verhey, *Great Reversal*; and more recently Ephrain Agosto, *Servant Leadership: Jesus and Paul* (St. Louis: Chalice, 2005).

39. So W. L. Lane, *The Gospel according to Mark*, NICNT (Grand Rapids: Eerdmans, 1974), 339.

that the specific action admonished in these texts is a particular manifestation of a more fundamental attitude, one that Jesus called the second-greatest commandment: love your neighbor as yourself. Returning to the theme of our study, Jesus' teachings about servant leadership have a clear and obvious translation into the ethics of roles. His commandments about authority and greatness may be summarized as: take up the role of a servant in order to be first and greatest in God's reign and realm (kingdom).

In another passage, this time from Mark 10, Jesus connects servant leadership more directly with true discipleship, that is, the way of the cross. Once again, the apostles are engaged in a disagreement about precedence and authority in the reign and realm of God. James and John want to sit on thrones of glory in the coming reign of God (10:35–40), but Jesus turns them down, for it is "not mine to grant" (v. 40). When the ten other apostles hear of this request, there is a real dustup! Jesus calls them together to teach them about leadership and authority. Among the Gentiles, the rulers "lord it over them," and "their great men exercise authority" (v. 42). Jesus rejects this common, worldly way of thinking about authority as a kind of hierarchy of "power-over." Instead, his disciples must be the servants of all: "whoever wants to be great among you must be your servant" and "whoever wants to be first [in precedence] among you must be the slave of all" (vv. 43, 44). In terms of the life, ministry, and teaching of Jesus, the reason for this utter change of attitude and behavior from man-centered hierarchies of power is absolutely decisive: "for even the Son of Man did not come to be served, but to serve, and to give his life as a ransom for many" (v. 45). The way of the cross is directly tied to taking up the role of a servant. Servant leadership is *the* sign of greatness and precedence in the reign and realm of God.

In the Synoptic Gospels, Jesus consistently teaches about authority in terms of taking up the role of a servant.[40] In Mark 10 he ties this servant role directly to his own example of giving his life freely, out of love, for his disciples. In the Gospel of John, he acts out this teaching in a symbolic or parabolic way. Jesus acts out the servant role for the disciples (and for us) in the famous passage about washing the disciples' feet during the Last Supper (John 13:1–20).[41] By depicting Jesus engaged in an activity usually performed by a lowly household slave, John emphasizes the power and authority of Jesus' servanthood at the start of this section of the narrative. Jesus "knew that his hour had come," when he was going to leave this world and return to the Father, and he knew "that the Father had given all things into his hands" (13:1, 3). Jesus loved his own "to the end" (that is, to death) and is about to demonstrate that love in his passion and crucifixion (see also John 15:13). Now, at the Last Supper, he will *enact* a parable to teach his disciples. The washing of the disciples' feet links the humiliation of Jesus freely giving his life for them on the cross with their continued act of service to one another. This was a physical cleansing of the feet that mirrored the cleansing power of his blood to wash away the stain of sin (13:10).[42] To follow Jesus is thus to walk in the way of the cross, a way of life that is a way of service: "If I your lord and teacher have washed your feet, then you should wash one another's feet. For I have given you an example, that you also should do as I have done to you" (13:14, 15). Linking this humble service directly to lordship and to his teaching, Jesus does not merely wash their feet but acts out a parable or

40. In addition to the passages mentioned in the text above, see Luke 9:46–48; 22:24–27; and Matthew 20:20–28.

41. For a careful analysis of this pericope, see Raymond Brown, *The Gospel according to John*, AB (Garden City, NY: Doubleday, 1966, 1970), 2:548–72.

42. Many commentators see the deeply symbolic parallel between this action at the Last Supper and Jesus' cleansing sacrifice at the cross, which was soon to take place. See, e.g., Brown, *John*, 558–64, who briefly reviews other options and argues that the footwashing was "a prophetic action symbolic of Jesus' death" (563).

metaphor for Christians in authority. True lordship in the realm of Jesus Christ is genuine, self-giving service. Authority shows itself in humble service to one another in the name of Jesus and out of love in the Spirit.

The washing of the disciples' feet in the Gospel of John is thus an enacted application of what Jesus consistently teaches in the first three Gospels about authority and precedence. To be a leader is to take up the role of a servant. With that in mind, we return to our basic question and are in a better position to answer it: does Christ submit to the church? The evidence from the Gospels and Epistles is clear and consistent: our answer depends on what one means by "submission." Christ does not and did not submit to the church if by "submission" we mean an external, involuntary obedience, or what we have called type I submission. But if we take up a different ethic of submission, one taught by Jesus himself, then *yes, Christ did submit to the church*. In his earthly ministry, humiliation, passion, and crucifixion, Christ voluntarily gave up power in order to take up the role of a slave, so as to serve the needs of his disciples. He not only washed their feet but also humbled himself and died for them on the cross. He consistently took up the role of a slave and lived out the ethics of mutual submission.

We have now come full circle. We can see that mutual submission or type II submission is exactly what Jesus taught and demonstrated in the name of servant leadership. Servant leadership is simply type II submission for those in leadership roles. Thus the argument that servant leadership is somehow different from mutual submission is profoundly unbiblical. To turn servant leadership into a kind of hierarchy of fixed authority is a sad misreading of the ethics of the New Testament. Such a conclusion is a deep misunderstanding of the teaching and example of Jesus Christ.

The sweeping claim just made cries out for further justification. Are there not other passages in the New Testament that do indeed teach a fixed hierarchy of power for men over women? What about the book of Genesis? In the next chapter we will examine just such passages to see whether mutual submission between men and women is indeed the consistent teaching of Scripture. We will discover that a Christ-centered, evangelical hermeneutic will clarify these passages and illuminate the consistent teaching of the Bible about the ethics of gender roles.

3

Mutual Submission
or Male Dominion?

Christ and Gender Roles in Ephesians
and 1 Corinthians

Before continuing our study of Scripture, let's take a brief look back at where we have been so far. Our task was to bring an evangelical approach to the question of the ethics of submission. Because evangelical faith is centered on the gospel of Jesus Christ, we look to Jesus to show us the meaning of both submission and leadership. Evangelicals will want to know what the whole of Scripture teaches on a topic before reaching conclusions about what these teachings mean today, since, after all, every part of the Bible is the Word of God written by human beings. Faithful Christian reading of Scripture demands that we read it as a whole canon. In our dialogue with the man-centered view of leadership and gender roles, we started to look at the ethics of roles. A careful study of certain New Testament texts in the Gospels and the Epistles gave us a profoundly coherent picture of the ethics of roles in leadership. To be a leader is to take up the role of a servant. We saw further that in Scripture there are two types of submission. The first type, which includes political and military meanings, is an external and involuntary submission that in practice is pretty much the same as obedience. The second type is more interpersonal. It is voluntary and is motivated by the internal desire of the one submitting to place the needs of the other before his or her own needs. It is this second type of submission that Jesus modeled and taught and that Christian leaders are called to enact. This is the kind of submission that can indeed be mutual and that Jesus himself practiced in relation to the church, according to John 13 and Philippians 2 (among other texts). We discovered, in short, that Christ did submit to the church and that he calls us to mutual submission in love toward one another.

In this chapter we transition from examining the ethics of roles to studying submission commands in the letters of the New Testament, starting with Ephesians 5:18–33. We will discover that in many cases submission is enjoined for missionary purposes rather than as a permanent hierarchy grounded in the will of God or the order of creation. In order to remain true to our principle of attending to the whole Word of God, we will also search the Scriptures to see if there is any basis for the claim that man-centered leadership is God's will or grounded in creation-order. But for this chapter, our focus is on Ephesians.

Ephesians 5 and Mutual Submission

At the heart of Ephesians 5:18–33 is what Paul calls a "mystery" (v. 32), and this mystery is part of an extended analogy.[1] In 5:21–33 Paul compares the union between husband and wife

---

1. My use of the name Paul to speak of the author is merely a convenience and a matter of tradition. Many scholars today dispute any direct Pauline authorship of Ephesians.

to the relationship between Christ and the church, the "bride of Christ." If we follow the logic of Paul's argument, and if we agree that what is being called for is a mutual submission between husband and wife, then by analogy the author must have in mind a kind of mutual submission between Christ and the church. This will be the conclusion of our exegetical argument in this section. My thesis is that yes, Paul does call for a mutual submission between Christ and the church, and this is one more outstanding reason why the only proper way to understand the ethics of Ephesians 5:21–33 is in terms of mutual submission.[2] My analysis of the passage has three parts. First I will make a brief argument in favor of finding mutual submission in Ephesians 5. This argument picks up on points already made above. Next I shall point to the analogy in the text between husband and wife, on the one hand, and Christ and his bride, the church, on the other. Finally I will argue that in the economy of salvation, Christ does indeed submit to the church. This analysis makes it even clearer that mutual submission, and not a top-down and permanent hierarchy, is the right way to understand this text for our times.

Husband and Wife, Christ and Church

For Paul, Christian marriage is one among many ways in which we live our life in Christ, always acting for him and to the glory of the Father. For example, a key passage dealing with male and female relationships in the Pauline Epistles, 1 Corinthians 11:2–16, makes a direct appeal to life "in the Lord"

2. The importance of the idea of mutual submission for understanding Ephesians 5:18–33 is argued in Barth, *Ephesians 4–6*, 608–753; Gilbert Bilezikian, *Beyond Sex Roles* (Grand Rapids: Baker Academic, 1985), 153–56; and Craig Keener, *Paul, Women and Wives* (Peabody, MA: Hendrickson, 1992), 155–67. See also I. H. Marshall, "Mutual Love and Submission in Marriage," in Pierce and Groothuis, *Discovering Biblical Equality*, 186–204. For an argument against mutual submission, see Grudem, *Evangelical Feminism and Biblical Truth*, 188–202. I respond to Grudem's argument at several points in the main text.

(v. 11). Ephesians 5 extends this appeal to a full-blown parallel with Christ and the church. Both texts refer us in some way to Christ, as one would expect in Pauline thought.

In Ephesians 5:21–33, Paul draws an extended analogy between husband and wife and Christ and his bride (or body, that is, the church). In the mystery of salvation, the unity of Christ and his bride is somehow parallel to the loving unity of "one flesh" shared between husband and wife. With many biblical scholars today, I would argue that Paul is enjoining a mutual submission between husband and wife in this passage. While there is no explicit command for the husband to submit, it is implied in the following admonitions:

- "Submit yourselves one to another, out of reverence [literally "fear"] for Christ." (v. 21)
- "Husbands, love your wives just as Christ has loved the church and gave himself for her." (v. 25)
- "Husbands ought to love their wives, for they are their own bodies." (v. 28)
- "Each of you must love his wife as he loves himself." (v. 33)

The fact that the whole pericope begins with "submit yourselves one to another, out of reverence for Christ" provides us with a central and essential understanding of submission as Paul is using it in this text. Paul calls on husbands to love their wives sacrificially, not to rule or govern them, as was commonly prescribed in the household codes of secular philosophers in the ancient world.[3] This powerful and repeated call for self-giving love of husbands toward their wives is rather unique in the cultural world of the New Testament.[4]

3. Keener, *Paul, Women and Wives*, 167.
4. This is why we cannot agree with Andrew Lincoln's conclusion that "despite its distinctively Christian elements, in terms of the actual roles it enjoins it [the Ephesian household code] falls well within normal expectations about the patriarchal household in the Greco-Roman world" (*Ephesians*, WBC [Waco: Word, 1990], 365). Lincoln

Some exegetes would demur at this point. They would point to the etymology and history of the word for submission, *hypotassomai*, as not allowing it to mean a mutual submission. We have already discussed and refuted this narrowing of the meaning of the term in the previous chapters of this book. Two points can be repeated here. First, etymology does not determine the meaning of a word. Usage determines the meaning of a word, both for a community of speakers and for an individual author. The origin of a term and its historical development do not determine the meaning a word may have in a particular passage. At best they can provide some illumination and a range of possible uses, but etymology is never decisive in establishing meaning. Second, the context of this verb in our passage is very different from the military and political context to which appeal is often made by those who insist that the only kind of submission is type I (external and involuntary). Secular usage cannot determine in advance the meaning of a term in the New Testament, although it obviously illuminates it. What matters is the usage in Ephesians 5:21 and the larger context of this verse in the epistle, which determine the verb's meaning for this passage. While in a military or political context *submission* can mean a freedom-destroying and permanent power over the one who must submit, this kind of type I submission is alien to the context of this passage. As we have already seen, one correct way to understand *hypotassomai* is "taking up the role of a servant." This meaning fits the context of our passage much better than a type I, top-down submission. We must remember that the pronoun "to one another" and the prepositional phrase "in the fear of Christ" influence the meaning of the verb "to submit" in decisive ways.

Christian mutual submission is a free and loving act by which we take up the role of a servant for our brother or sisters as a

mentions but does not draw out the significance of the fact that Christ is servant to the church in his interpretation of the passage (366).

means of discipleship in Christ. This definition implies that the
submission is not permanent, nor is it one-way. Thus husbands
and wives should yield to one another, as the need arises, out
of love. Indeed, this is a common Pauline claim concerning the
ethical behavior of all Christians in relation to one another. In
Galatians 5:13, for example, Christians are called to be slaves to
one another (that is, to take on the role of a servant out of love
for one's brother or sister in Christ): "For you were called to
freedom, brothers and sisters; only do not use your freedom as an
opportunity for self-indulgence, but through love become slaves
to one another" (NRSV). Note that the pronoun "one another"
(*allelous*) means that not just some groups of Christians, but
all Christians, are to be slaves to one another through love. The
same basic ethical position is found in Philippians 2:3–4: "Do
nothing from selfishness or empty conceit, but with humility of
mind regard one another as more important than yourselves;
do not [only] look out for your own personal interests, but also
for the interests of others." By using "one another" three times
in Ephesians 4 (vv. 2, 25, 32), Paul sets up the central theme of
this passage, namely, the mutual submission of all Christians
to each other.[5] "One another" in Ephesians 4 and 5 does not
refer to just a few Christians but to the whole church. There
is no permanent role-hierarchy in the church of one Christian
over another, or of husbands over wives. Rather, as Paul says in
Ephesians 4:2, we are to live "with all humility and gentleness,
with patience, bearing with one another in love" (NRSV). Do
only some Christians bear with some others? Does not Paul
obviously mean that all Christians bear with all others? Those
who argue differently may be allowing their theology to dictate
what the text must mean in advance.

5. But cf. O'Brien, *Letter to the Ephesians*, 398–405, who argues that "one another"
is only some Christians to other Christians (not all to all), and that "submission"
always means a role-hierarchical, top-down relationship. I suggest above some reasons
why this view is dubious. See also Marshall, "Mutual Love," 196–97.

Does Christ Submit to the Church?

We now come to the heart of the matter. Ephesians repeatedly draws on Christ and the church for its theology and ethics, and chapter 5 is no exception. There is an extended analogy between Christ and the church and husband and wife in this passage that grounds the following argument: if Paul is calling for a mutual submission between husband and wife, and if there is a clear and profound analogy drawn with Christ and his bride, the church, it follows that Christ must also submit to the church. This argument from analogy seems correct. If Ephesians 5 really does enjoin mutual submission between husband and wife, it must also be suggesting by analogy a mutual submission between the church and its head, Jesus Christ.

I will now prove from Scripture that Christ does indeed submit to the church when this submission is understood as mutual—namely, in taking up the role of a servant or slave. We have analyzed mutual submission as a temporary and free gift of service, the taking up of the role of a servant out of self-giving love in order to meet the needs of the other. The notion of mutual submission does not imply that this servanthood will endure for a long time, or that somehow this submission is natural, created by God, or God's permanent command. It is not a service that is imposed by nature or by any external authority. One who serves today may well be served tomorrow. As Aristotle remarks regarding political relationships within a democracy of equal citizens, "In most constitutional states the citizens rule and are ruled by turns, for the idea of a constitutional state implies that the natures of the citizens are equal, and do not differ at all."[6] I am not arguing that Christ submits to the church in a permanent role-hierarchy but rather that Jesus took up freely and lovingly the role of a servant during his earthly ministry for the benefit of all who believe on his name.

6. Aristotle, *Politics* 1.11.1259B.

Perhaps the most striking narrative demonstrating Christ's submission to the church is his washing the disciples' feet in John's Gospel, a passage we have already mentioned. In John 13:3–17 Jesus takes up a role reserved for slaves in the ancient world. In other words, Jesus becomes a servant to the disciples. He then draws this conclusion (13:13–14): "You call me teacher and Lord, and you are right for so I am. If then I, your Lord and teacher, have washed your feet, so you ought to wash one another's feet." Just as the Lord has taken up the role of a servant toward the disciples, so they in turn ought mutually to serve one another. It is not impossible that in the deeply symbolic narrative world of John's Gospel, this footwashing is a sign of Christ washing away our sins and thus points to his imminent death on the cross.

We have already found the same ethic of mutual submission enjoined in the Synoptic Gospels, but in different terms. In discussing the authority his disciples will have in the reign and realm of God, Jesus specifically rejects any kind of "lording it over" or exercising authority over one another: "It shall not be so among you; but whoever would be great among you must be your servant, and whoever would be first among you must be slave of all" (Mark 10:43–44). Jesus then turns to himself as an example of this kind of servanthood under the title Son of Man: "For the Son of Man also came not to be served but to serve, and to give his life as a ransom for many" (10:45). Jesus takes up the role of slave or servant to the "many" by giving his life as a ransom for their sins.

Again, as already argued in this book, the same point is taken up in a different way in the Christ hymn in Philippians 2. There we read that, even though Jesus was "in the form of God," he did not hold on to his godly authority but humbled himself and took up the "form of a slave." He "became obedient to the point of death, even death on a cross" (2:6–8). The key question here is, to whom did Jesus become a slave? To whom did Jesus submit? The text itself does not say, and any specific answer will be speculative. For our purposes, what is important is the parallelism of the two phrases in verse 7: "taking the form of a slave" and "being born in human likeness." In becoming incarnate, the Son also freely takes up the role of a servant. This role is, however, only a temporary one, for now Jesus is the highly exalted Lord of all. And in the larger context of the chapter, Jesus' example becomes the basis for the teaching about mutual submission among believers in Philippians 2:1–4.

Is it true that there is a mutual submission between Christ and the church? Does Christ ever submit to the church? The answer of the New Testament is yes. Jesus submits to the church by freely becoming a servant in his earthly ministry, especially in his passion and death for us. This is a mutual submission, not a permanent and external subordination. This loving service by Christ for humans can be found by those with eyes to see in Ephesians 5 as well. After calling for husbands to love their wives, Paul writes that this should be done "as Christ loved the church and gave himself up for her" (5:25). Jesus makes his bride holy and washes her "with the word," which makes her clean (5:26, a reference to being cleansed from sin). Here we find an echo of the Gospel narratives, in which Christ takes up the role of a servant in order to wash away or redeem us from the stain of sin. I have argued that this self-giving love, even unto death on a cross, is in fact the sort of mutual submission that Paul enjoins in Ephesians 5:21. The consistent teaching of the New Testament is that Jesus has indeed taken up the role of a servant out of love for us. A relationship of mutual submission exists between Christ and his bride, the church; therefore we should now love and serve one another out of reverence for this Lord who is also a servant. I thus conclude that mutual submission is the proper interpretation of the submission of wives to their husbands enjoined in Ephesians 5:21–33.

Objections Considered

What objections could possibly be brought to this interpretation? The fact that the exact words "husbands, submit to your
wives" do not occur in the text is rather superficial and can be
ignored as unimportant and uninteresting. The rhetorical power
of this passage for husbands in a patriarchal society would
have been greatly weakened by such blunt commands; Paul's
purpose in moving them from patriarchy to mutuality would
have been undermined.

A more significant objection has to do with the Greek word
kephalē. Since Jesus is ontologically head of the church, an
objector might say that he is always and everywhere Lord and
ruler, one who deserves our total submission and obedience.
This ontological hierarchy cannot be reversed because it is for-
ever grounded in who we are and who he is. At best, the loving
service of Christ can show us how men should be leaders—that
is, in a gentle and loving manner. So Jesus cannot be one who
really submits to us.

This objection seems sound at first glance, but upon careful
reflection it is quite flawed. This understanding of lordship
and headship is exactly what Jesus himself rejects. Too much is
read into the term *kephalē*, which in fact has a wide variety of
meanings as a metaphor. Recently Richard Cervin and Andrew
Perriman have argued that the diverse metaphorical meanings
of *kephalē* can be grouped around the idea of being first or
preeminent in some way, including being the source of something.[7] Those who think *kephalē* always means "authority" in
Paul (while allowing it may also mean "origin") have not read
1 Corinthians 11:2–16 carefully enough. In 1 Corinthians 11:3
the meaning is obviously one of origin, and not authority, as
11:8–9 makes clear. The word *head* should also be understood

7. R. S. Cervin, "Does *Kephalē* Mean 'Source' or 'Authority Over' in Greek Literature? A Rebuttal," *TJ*, n.s., 10 (1989): 85–112; A. Perriman, "The Head of a Woman,"
JTS 45 (1994): 602–22.

as "source" or "origin" in Colossians 2:10, in which Paul speaks of Jesus as "the head of all rule and authority." *Kephalē* in this verse cannot mean "authority" in and of itself; otherwise Paul would just be repeating himself with three words. Rather, it means that Christ is the *origin* or *source* of all rule and authority. Let's take an example of my point. If my garden hose is the source of all the water in my backyard, it cannot itself also be water. The "source" of the water does not mean water itself; and referring to Christ as the *kephalē* of all authority does not mean "authority," but rather "source." For the concept of lordship in this verse, Paul uses the terms *archē* and *exousia*, which are properly understood as "authority" or "rule." The only unambiguous place in Pauline literature in which *kephalē* means "authority" is Ephesians 1:22; but it does not have this meaning in Ephesians 4:15–16, where Christ as head is the unifying source of the body (that is, the church). In any case, *kephalē* in Ephesians 5:21–33 most certainly does not mean "lordship" in any plain and simple sense. In this passage, Jesus is the head of the church by taking care of his bride, not by lording over her. Jesus takes the lead (*kephalē*) in being a servant, and his headship is not a role-hierarchy. This lord is also a servant, and this servant is also the Lord. Christians do indeed submit to Jesus, just as wives should submit to husbands; but Jesus has also submitted to us in love and taken up the role of a slave for us in the economy of salvation history. Husbands should do likewise in relation to their wives. Free, loving, and mutual submission is the way of following after Jesus in true discipleship.

We have seen in this key passage of Ephesians 5 that the best way to understand the marriage ethic of submission is to accept the analogy Paul draws between Christ and his bride, on the one hand, and husband and wife, on the other. I have shown from Scripture that Christ did indeed submit to the church freely, out of love, so that now the church should submit to Christ. I have shown that the best sense of *submission* in Ephesians 5:21 is taking up the role of a servant. Thus for biblically minded theologians, mutual submission is the clear ethical implication of this passage for today. The man-centered ethics of role-hierarchy founders not only on this text but also on the example and teaching of Jesus himself.

Sex at Corinth: Gender Roles in 1 Corinthians

Of all Paul's letters, 1 Corinthians deals most with issues of gender and sexuality. The reason for this is obvious to anyone who has studied the letter. The new Christians at Corinth, drawn from many walks of life and many cultures, had a number of serious problems that Paul has to correct in this letter. The apostle consistently refers to life together in Christ as the basis for his theological and ethical admonitions. What he has to say about women, men, and gender roles is just one part of his larger argument, yet our focus will be on them. In particular, we will look at issues of headship and submission in this letter.[8]

1 Corinthians 6–7

Paul's theology of marriage is drawn from Judaism and the Old Testament but transformed by his Christ-centered theology. In 1 Corinthians 6:16 Paul quotes the same phrase from Genesis 2:24 we have already noted from our study of Ephesians 5: "the two shall become one flesh." In the context of sexual immorality at Corinth, Paul insists that sexual intercourse is a binding, unifying act. It is meant for marriage, not for the bed of a prostitute. By going to prostitutes, therefore, the Corin-

8. This section is based on research previously published in several of my articles in academic journals: "Paul on Women in the Church: The Contradictions of Coiffure in 1 Corinthians 11.2–16," *JSNT* 20 (1984): 69–86; "Feminism in First Corinthians: A Dialogue with Elisabeth Schüssler Fiorenza," *EvQ* 58 (1986): 121–32; and "The Significance of ἀντί in 1 Corinthians 11:15," *TynBul* 45 (1994): 181–87. Further bibliographic sources and dialogue with other scholars can be found in them.

thians were "sinning against [their] own body" (6:18). What is more, they were sinning against Christ himself, since they were "one spirit with him" through faith (6:17). For this reason, Paul argues, "your [plural] body is a temple of the Holy Spirit" and should not be defiled with sexual immorality (6:19). Obviously the Corinthians were having issues with the ethics of sex, and Paul addresses their immoral behavior from his Christ-centered theology of discipleship.

Continuing on to discuss problems with gender at Corinth, Paul mentions a letter he had received from the church (7:1). With many scholars today, I believe several phrases in this letter are not from Paul himself but rather are quotations or allusions to the Corinthian viewpoint. Examples include 6:12, "All things are lawful to me," and the phrase in 7:1 that has been so influential among monks throughout the church's history: "It is good for a man not to touch a woman." Like Jesus, Paul was single and celibate—a very unusual practice among Jewish men of their time. Most Jewish men, and especially rabbis, would be expected to marry and bear children as part of their obedience to God. So Paul, a single man, must now speak of the importance of marriage to one party at Corinth that was in doubt about Christians engaging in sex at all. We might say they had the opposite problem of the ones who were going to prostitutes!

It is in the midst of correcting Corinthian misunderstanding that Paul very clearly sets forth an egalitarian view of the role relationships between women and men: "The husband ought to give himself to his wife, and the wife to her husband. The wife does not have power over her own body, but the husband does; so also the husband does not have power over his own body but the wife does" (7:3–4). Such full equality in teaching about marriage is very unusual for Paul's time, whether among Greek philosophers or Jewish theologians. Nevertheless, he is very careful in this chapter to balance what he has to say about sex and marriage in reference to both single and married people, and to both women and men.

This strong egalitarian remark is not just a one-off comment. It is grounded in Galatians 3:28, where Paul declares that all believers (male or female, Jew or Greek, slave or free) are one in Christ. But Paul's theology of equal sharing in marriage is not limited to Galatians 3 or 1 Corinthians 7. He makes exactly the same point in 1 Corinthians 11.

1 Corinthians 11

First Corinthians 11:2–16 is a difficult passage for any interpreter.[9] But some parts are clear enough, and we do not need to understand every detail of the passage to get the main point. There seems to have been a debate between the Corinthians and Paul over the meaning of "head" (11:3) and the proper use of head-coverings for women and men during the worship service (11:4–10). After making his points in the debate, Paul summarizes what is most important to him, starting with the word *plēn* ("nevertheless," "however"). Let us focus for now on this part of the passage, a part that sounds very much like 1 Corinthians 7: "Nevertheless, in the Lord woman is not independent from man nor is man independent from woman. For just as woman was from man, so also the man is from the woman; and all people come from God" (vv. 11–12). We need to interpret this text in its context just a bit. As we just noted, the passage as a whole is about headship and head-covering for men and women in church. Paul begins by speaking about "head" in a way that is unusual for him; it is very likely that once again he is interacting with Corinthian teachings. We noticed before that the word *kephalē* ("head") can have a wide variety of meanings, including that of a literal head. Paul's concern in this context is not about *authority* but about *origin*: who comes

9. See chapter 5 of this book for my proposed reading of the passage.

from whom? This concern seems to be at the root of his debate with the Corinthians. In 11:11–12 Paul makes the whole argument appear to be of little importance "in the Lord." After all, not only did Eve come from the side of Adam in the creation story, but now men come from women by birth, and all *people* come from God. Most translations have this final phrase as "all things come from God," but the debate is about where people come from, so we should translate it as I just have: "all *people* come from God." All people come from God, and all people are made in the image of God, as Genesis teaches (1:27). So questions of who comes from whom are not of any deep significance for those in Christ. The egalitarian character of this passage is quite striking, especially in the context of the larger argument about head-coverings and headship.

It is true that in his debate with the Corinthians, Paul wrote that the man (male) "is the image and glory of God, but woman is the glory of man" (11:7). The argument here is difficult, and scholars cannot agree on how to interpret it. But we don't need to make a decision about that here. What we can take away from our brief look at a complex passage is that (1) the metaphorical sense of "head" can be about origin and is not always about authority; and (2) Paul held that even though man is the head of woman, nevertheless, such issues of headship are overcome *in the Lord*. Just how Paul thought this was overcome in practice, as I have come to read this passage, is found in 11:10: because woman is the glory of man, "for this reason she ought to have authority over her [literal] head." In other words, women ought to have what they did not have according to some Corinthian leaders—that is, the power to wear or not wear a head-covering in church when they pray or prophesy. While I have a definite view of the best way to interpret this passage, we will return to it later and press on now to what is no doubt the best-known Corinthian passage on women and submission, 1 Corinthians 14:34–35.

1 Corinthians 14

Experts in textual criticism have long suggested that 1 Corinthians 14:34–35 may not have been part of the original letter written by Paul. Beginning with "the women" of verse 34,
some ancient manuscripts move these sentences to the end of
the chapter.[10] While a sound argument can be made for this
view, for the purposes of the present discussion we will accept
the passage as original. I am convinced that these verses are
original because the structure of the command to "be quiet"
follows the same pattern as the other two authentic ones (as I
will soon explain). This would be quite a feat for a secondary
insertion by a later copyist. What is more, I would argue that
the follow-up command in 14:38 was written directly to the
women in question in 14:34–35. If my reading of 14:38—which
I will defend shortly—is correct, then the previous verses must
be original.

The context of 1 Corinthians 14 is a larger debate about
spiritual gifts in the letter (chaps. 12–14). Paul's main concern
in this passage as a whole is for decency and order in the worship service (14:40). He uses an extended, beautiful metaphor
in these chapters in which the gifts of the Spirit are likened to
music (13:1; 14:7–8). This metaphor is based in part on the
root meaning of the word *spirit* in the Bible, which comes from
words for breath or wind. God the Holy Spirit is the conductor
of the worship service, and the vocal gifts stem from the breath
of God. They are a gift of the Spirit and so are meant to edify
the church and glorify God (14:2–4, 26). The problem is that
the gifts of the Spirit at Corinth were being used in ways that
disrupted the order and edification of the worship service. Paul's
overall concern in the passage is decency, order, and peace in
the service out of respect and awe for God: "For God is a God
of peace, as in all the churches of the saints" (14:33). Paul does

10. See the brief discussion in Bruce M. Metzger, *A Textual Commentary on the
Greek New Testament*, 2nd ed. (New York: United Bible Societies, 1994), 499–500.

not tell only women to "be silent" in this chapter; rather, he tells *three* groups of those who were speaking in church to be silent (14:26–33). The verb and the structure of the command are the same in all three cases: (1) the group is identified, (2) they are told to "be quiet" (*sigatō*), and (3) some reason for their silence is given. Let us look at each group in turn.

Those who speak in tongues are called to be silent when there is no one to interpret the tongue-speaking. The reason for this is the focus on edification: if no one can understand the tongue-speaker, the body of Christ is not built up in worship (14:26–28). The same concern for decency, order, and peace in the worship service is applied by the apostle to prophets. Those who have a prophetic revelation from God should speak one at a time. If someone new has just received a prophetic word, the first one should be silent and let the other speak: "If a revelation is made to another sitting by, let the first prophet be silent. For you can all prophesy one by one, so that all may learn and be encouraged" (14:30–31). Note again the emphasis on edification and order in the service.

The third group called to silence is women. This group is not composed of all women all the time but rather of specific women who were asking questions and speaking in the service. The larger context of these verses demands that we understand these questioning women to be a disruption of the peace and order of the service. This is the reason Paul wrote that "women should keep silent in the churches" (v. 34). Paul's concern is not just with women (for men too are called to be silent in church); his broader concern is with silence, peace, and order in the worship assembly. This perspective allows us rightly to understand the rest of this chapter, 14:34–40. Paul next tells these specific women to "be in submission." We tend to think of this as submission *to men*, but the larger context makes this improbable. Our patriarchal and man-centered culture over the millennia has distorted the meaning of this command to submit. Rather than commanding submission to men, the apostle is commanding *submission to the order of the worship service*, that is, submission to the Holy Spirit. This reading helps us understand the next phrase: "even as the law says." Normally *law* in Paul refers to the Old Testament, but it can also have a wider meaning. Nowhere in the Old Testament are women called to be silent, nor are they called to submit to their husbands.[11] Yet there is excellent evidence for biblical and broadly Jewish concern for *silence in worship* before God or the Word of God, or while learning from the rabbis (e.g., Deut. 27:9–10; Job 33:31–33; Isa. 66:2; Hab. 2:20).[12] It may well be that this is the "law" Paul has in mind: not about the silence or submission of women, but about silence in the worship service in general (but applying it to women in this case).

Viewed in this light, silence is a positive, spiritual sense of peace, reflection, and "fear of the Lord" rather than a mere shutting up. This kind of silence included silence before and during the hearing of the biblical text and the preaching or teaching of the rabbi. Those learning wisdom were expected to keep silent. An example is the saying of Rabbi Akiba, a contemporary of Paul: "The tradition is a fence around the Law; tithes are a fence around riches; vows are a fence around abstinence; a fence around wisdom is silence."[13] Understood in context, the women at Corinth were not being commanded never to speak, nor were they being called to submit to men. Rather, their submission was to the peace and order of worship, to the Spirit, and to the Word of God. As Paul says in Romans 8:7, "The carnal mind is hostile to God, for it does not submit to the law of God." Just so, these women were not obeying the law of silence before the worship and Word of God.

11. As we shall see in the next chapter, Genesis 3:15 is not a command for women to submit to their husbands.

12. See Aída Besançon Spencer, *Beyond the Curse: Women Called to Ministry* (Nashville: Thomas Nelson, 1985), 76–81.

13. Ibid., 78, citing the Mishnah at *m. Avot* 3:14.

Paul's next sentence gives the concrete details of this wrong kind of unspiritual talk in which the women were engaging: "If there is anything they desire to know," he enjoins, "let them ask their husbands at home" (v. 35). Women were attracted to the new religion of Jesus Christ, and were often quite uneducated and illiterate in the ancient world. They no doubt had much they wished to learn and many questions. But their unspiritual talk was interrupting the service and did not edify the body. Therefore they must remain silent, speak only when appropriate, and ask their questions later of their husbands at home.

Next we find another famous remark that on the surface seems antiwoman: "For it is shameful for a woman to speak in church" (v. 35). In the larger context of silence and peace in worship, and of women who were asking questions that interrupted the flow of the Spirit, we can see where this public shame comes from. Paul does not mean that it is shameful for any woman ever to speak in church. Rather, it is shameful for *these* women to speak *in this way* in the church service. The silence of these women gives honor to God; their disruptive speaking brings shame to them and to the body at worship.

Paul's concern for reverence, silence, and peace during worship comes out in his next rhetorical remark: "What? Has the word of God originated with you, or are you the only ones it has reached?" (v. 36). He is seeking to shame those who press themselves forward with their own speech, interrupting the due reverence of God and God's Word. With this question he returns to thinking of all three groups: women, prophets, and tongue-speakers. Those who are prophets or "spiritual" should know that Paul's restrictions are a command from the Lord and not mere human wisdom (v. 37). He explicitly discusses prophets and those who speak in tongues in 14:37–40; but does he forget the talkative women? I think not, but English translations and traditional interpretations have obscured this point.

I argued above that Paul calls on these Corinthian women to keep silent, to learn in wisdom rather than engage in disruptive questioning, and to be in submission to the Spirit's leading in the assembly at worship. This concern comes back again in 14:38: "If anyone does not recognize this [command], let *her* be ignored." The last phrase of this sentence is a single verb in Greek, *agnoeitai*, the passive form of the verb "to not know, to be ignorant." It is usually translated "let him be ignored" and interpreted as a man being ignored by either God or the church. However, the original Greek allows for any gender: him, her, or it. Since Paul is summing up here, and mentions again both prophets and tongue-speakers, it is likely he would mention the women again. That he would do so here makes excellent sense: it is not a *he* that should be ignored, but rather a *she*—specifically, the kind of woman called to be silent earlier in the chapter. In other words, the questions of these women should be ignored if they refuse to recognize the wisdom of silence. This reading of *agnoeitai* is a natural one for the Greek verb and the context, making better sense than the usual interpretation. Why a *man* should be ignored for not recognizing Paul's command has yet to be explained clearly. The alternative of a *woman* being ignored (that is, her questions) has been overlooked simply because of male-centered interpretations and translations, which assume that "anyone" must be "he."

Conclusion

Having indulged in some detailed examination of these passages from 1 Corinthians, we now need to step back and look at the big picture. We began this chapter by arguing for mutual submission between husbands and wives in Ephesians 5. The fact that man is "head" of woman does not imply authority over so much as it implies *being first* in some way. Sometimes this language does have overtones of authority, but that is not the main point of the text, which is primarily written to husbands. We found in 1 Corinthians 7 another example of Paul's teaching concerning mutual submission for husbands and wives living together as "one flesh." As such, they each have authority over the body of their mate. The mutuality of man and woman "in the Lord" was also found in 1 Corinthians 11. While Paul does call on women to be silent and to submit in 1 Corinthians 14, we have seen that this chapter is about order in worship and silence in learning, not the submission of women to men.

So far we have found little reason to affirm a fixed hierarchy of men over women in Paul's letters; but we have found several texts that point in a very different direction. As in the Gospels, mutual submission is the rule, at least so far. Of course there are other New Testament texts outside of the Gospels, Galatians, Philippians, Ephesians, and 1 Corinthians dealing with issues of submission and gender roles. These other texts are later in the history of the New Testament, written during a time of greater emphasis on church organization in an era of persecution and a parallel concern with false teachers. These later texts, especially 1 Timothy 2, are the ones that man-centered church leaders will point to in justification of their view of submission as a fixed, top-down hierarchy of roles, with men at the top. Studying them will also require a brief study of the early chapters of Genesis. Overall we will discover once again that there is no basis in Scripture for a fixed hierarchy of roles for women and men. There is no solid biblical basis for a "creation-order" of husband over wife. This does not mean there are no biblical passages about wives submitting to husbands, or men being the "head." There are! The debate concerning theories of male dominion is about the theological justification of such submission and the larger question of how such passages are to be understood and lived out in the church today. To these later passages we now turn.

4

Mission and Submission

1 Peter and the Pastoral Epistles

Our argument so far has been about submission and gender roles. In the Gospels and several key New Testament
letters, submission is understood not merely as a top-down,
involuntary obedience. Rather, following the model of Jesus,
Christian submission is a voluntary self-giving in love, which
should be thought of first as a *role* rather than a social institution. Of course role and institution are not totally separate, but
the emphasis in servant leadership is on the concrete, specific
act ("role") that can be understood as taking up the role of a
servant. We also discovered that between men and women the
ideal is one of mutual submission, of which servant leadership
is a type. For the New Testament ethic so far examined, "in the
Lord" woman and man, husband and wife, are not independent but one flesh; they show their love in the context of society
through mutual submission and servant leadership (when in a
leadership role).

As we move further along in the history of the New Testament era, we enter into a slightly different context for understanding later letters, and in particular their ethic of submission.[1] Instead of the mutual submission we found in Galatians, Ephesians, and Philippians, in 1 Peter and the Pastoral Epistles (1–2 Timothy, Titus) the emphasis is on the inferior members, those with a lower social status. Concern for the whole household is almost completely absent, so that moral remarks to children and parents simply drop out. What has happened?

The early and rather small Jesus movement has begun to grow and to encounter opposition. Some of this opposition is internal, especially in the form of false teachers and alternative leadership. The concern with false teachers is particularly prominent in the Pastorals, as we will see. Equally distressing was the growing opposition to the Way (as Christians called their movement early on; see Acts 9:2; 19:23) from local communities of Jewish leaders and Roman citizens. While these letters are too early to know of widespread, official imperial persecution, local opposition to the new faith was growing. Both 1 Peter and the Pastorals are concerned with the reputations of Christians in the arena of public opinion. First Peter in particular is written to a community undergoing suffering for the gospel. The text is best understood in a larger social context of suffering under persecution and concern for the external reputation of Christians among outsiders who could and did bring accusations of wrongdoing against members of this new and illegal sect. This is quite clear in the texts themselves, although the importance of this context for understanding the ethic of submission in these letters has often been overlooked.[2]

1. My thinking on this topic was influenced early in my research by Peter Lippert, *Leben als Zeugnis* (Stuttgart: Katholisches Bibelwerk, 1968), which is a study of 1 Peter and the Pastorals. See further the next footnote.

2. See A. G. Padgett, "The Pauline Rationale for Submission: Biblical Feminism and the *hina* Clauses of Titus 2:1–10," *EvQ* 59 (1987): 39–52, for scholarly bibliography and discussion. Important books that influenced my understanding of these texts

Submission and the Outsider in 1 Peter

Peter knows that the church lives in exile or diaspora in the Roman Empire ("Babylon" is Rome; 1 Pet. 5:13). During this early period, Christians are a small minority and have serious opponents in their local communities; but the hope of the church is still strong since it is founded in Jesus, his resurrection, and his second coming. For this reason, Christians should be willing to undergo suffering for what is right, since they have such a solid hope: "Now for a little while you have to suffer affliction in various trials," which is a test of faith in Jesus and his salvation (1:6–7). The ethics of 1 Peter focus on "doing good"—that is, on holiness in behavior (1:15–16; 2:9)—not only as a result of faith and the imitation of Jesus but also to put the lie to any accusations of Christian wrongdoing. Peter's ethic of Christian submission is a broad one that applies to all Christians who live in exile in this world: "Beloved, I urge you as aliens and exiles to refrain from the passions of the flesh that wage war against your soul. Keep up your good conduct among the nations [or Gentiles], so that when they speak against you as wrongdoers, they may see your good works and glorify God on the day of visitation" (2:11–12).

It is in the larger context of concern for the moral judgment of outsiders that Peter goes on immediately to command: "Be in submission for the Lord's sake to every human institution, whether to the emperor as supreme, or to governors as sent by him to punish those who do wrong and praise those who do right" (2:13–14). The first concern of this text is *submission to the emperor* and the Roman imperial officers. Given the imperial

---

include Lippert, *Leben als Zeugnis*, and David L. Balch, *Let Wives Be Submissive: The Domestic Code in 1 Peter* (Chino, CA: Scholars Press, 1981). A fine study by Peter H. Towner, *The Goal of Our Instruction* (Sheffield: Sheffield Academic Press, 1989), was published after my article originally appeared. Towner went on to write an excellent commentary as well: *The Letters to Timothy and Titus*, NICNT (Grand Rapids: Eerdmans, 2006).

and political context, this makes sense as a kind of type I submission—that is, obedience to an external authority. Yet the concern is not so much political as it is evangelical and apologetic. Peter is concerned with the moral opinion of outsiders who could and did persecute and slander Christians: "For it is God's will that by doing right you should put to silence the ignorance of fools" (2:15). Still, Peter wants the reader to bring a Christlike attitude to this kind of submission. This is clear in the text as a whole and in the long explanation given for the submission of slaves. So even type I submission is given a larger, Christ-centered meaning.

After calling all Christians to submit to imperial authorities, Peter moves to the slaves. No reference is made here to the right behavior of Christian masters, such as we find in other texts (e.g., Col. 4:1). Peter is concerned primarily with forms of disobedience to social institutions that would bring immediate, perhaps even violent, condemnation by the Romans. He wants the public reputation of Christian faith to be above reproach. So, first, Christians must obey the emperor.

Christian slaves could also bring greater opportunity for slander and persecution if they were disobedient; thus slaves must be submissive "not only to the kind and gentle but also to the domineering" (2:18). Masters here are not addressed as part of the Christian community; a Christian slave may well be punished unjustly, as slaves often were. The immediate reason Peter gives for suffering even when the slave is innocent and did no wrong is the passion of Christ: "Christ also suffered for you, leaving you an example, so that you may follow in his steps" (2:21). What we see here is a *one-sided* application of the ethic of servant leadership we discovered in the Gospels and other Epistles. There is no moral command to those in power to be loving, self-giving, and caring toward other sisters and brothers in Christ—no injunction to use power as a way to empower others. The context of this letter demands an ethic of external and one-sided obedience, not mutual submission.

Peter applies this same ethic to Christian wives. Wives should submit to their husbands "so that some, though they do not obey the Word, may be won without a word by the behavior of their wives" (3:1). The function of good Christian behavior goes beyond the avoidance of slander (see also 3:15) toward a positive witness. There is also an evangelistic purpose at work, although it is muted for the most part. We will see this evangelical or missionary motive demonstrated more fully in the Pastorals. Here in 1 Peter 3 there is a brief discussion of the right behavior of husbands toward wives (3:7) that echoes the teaching to Christian households in other letters; but the focus is on the submission of *believing* wives to *unbelieving* husbands. The concern for Christians under persecution and the judgment of outsiders against the new faith motivates the ethic of humble submission to human institutions, including the patriarchy of the Roman household. Peter is also concerned to make the new faith attractive to those who may yet come to believe: "Always be prepared to make a defense" of your faith to those who oppose the gospel; but live a good and unblemished life "so that when you are abused those who revile your good behavior in Christ may be put to shame" (3:15–16). Alongside this concern for outsiders exists, as one would expect, a general Christian motivation to live holy lives because God is holy—to live out the faith without fear from persecution, suffering for his sake and "reverencing Christ as Lord in your hearts" (3:15). First Peter does not ignore Jesus as a motive for Christian discipleship! Yet the concern for outsiders in the midst of Christian suffering is also evident.

A good argument can be made, therefore, that the submission of wives to husbands prescribed in 1 Peter 3 is *not* mutual; this is a form not of type II submission, but of type I. Wives and slaves do not willingly take up the role of a servant out of love on a temporary basis; rather, the Roman hierarchy of empire and family patriarchy is here held up as something for

Christians to submit to as an external authority. This hierarchy includes the social authority of husbands and masters in the Roman household.

We have seen that the ethic of submission in 1 Peter is best understood in its original social and political context of persecution and accusation by unbelievers. This best explains its one-sided application of the ethics of mutual submission found in earlier and better-known New Testament books. For these reasons, it would be a strange argument indeed that concluded that 1 Peter's one-sided ethic of submission is normative for wives in every time and place, rather than the mutual submission and servant leadership (type II submission) we find in the teachings of Jesus and in the earlier letters.

Submission and the Beauty of the Gospel: Titus 2 and 1 Timothy 6

When we move to the last of the letters bearing Paul's name, the so-called Pastoral Epistles, we are also moving into the later period of New Testament times. Although Titus and 1–2 Timothy are distinct works, their similar style, concerns, theology, and probable dating (around the time of the death of Paul?) have placed them together in the minds of modern scholars. Together we now call them "pastoral" epistles. While the other letters of Paul are listed by size in the Bible, these are placed just before the short Philemon, at the end of our canonical list of Pauline letters. They have a unity in the thought of whoever put Paul's letters together as a collection. Both Titus and 1 Timothy show a concern for the opinion of outsiders similar to that of 1 Peter, and both date from a similar time. But added to this is a strong concern for false teaching or heresy in the churches of Crete (Titus) and Ephesus (Timothy). The longest of these epistles, 1 Timothy, starts right out with this central concern—namely, leaders in the church who are teaching "different doctrine" filled with "myths and genealogies that promote speculations rather than the divine plan of faith" (1:3–4). Likewise, in the opening chapter of Titus the young missionary pastor is warned of "insubordinate people, empty talkers and deceivers, especially those of the circumcision group" (1:10). Titus is to teach the Cretans sound or healthy doctrine, "instead of holding to Jewish myths or the commands of people who reject the truth" (1:14). A similar concern can be found in Paul's charge and advice to his closest follower and fellow missionary, Timothy (2 Tim. 2:14–18; 3:13). Thus unlike 1 Peter (but like 2 Peter, 1 John, and other letters), the Pastoral Epistles give strong evidence of false teachers within the churches at Crete and Ephesus. These alternative Christian leaders were tempting believers away from sound teachings grounded in the gospel of Christ. This is not the only motive for these three letters, but it was a powerful one among others.

Like the submission ethics of 1 Peter, the ethics of Titus and 1 Timothy call Christians to submit for reasons other than a fundamental Christ-following ethic of submission (that is, mutual love and care expressed in taking up the role of a slave). Slaves, wives, young people, older men, and widows are addressed not as members of a Christian family but as public citizens of the Roman Empire whose conduct will be scrutinized by their unbelieving neighbors. The concern for outsiders and the public reputation of the Christian faith once again comes through, sometimes with a strongly worded rationale: "Let all who are under the yoke of slavery regard their masters as worthy of all honor, *so that* the name of God and the teachings will not be blasphemed" (1 Tim. 6:1). The name of God and divine teaching will be blasphemed by unbelievers if they associate Christian faith with insubordinate slaves. This problem is in fact a kind of reverse compliment to the new religion, which gave slaves a reason to feel fully human. They were at one even with free citizens who were fellow believers because all are one in Christ

(Gal. 3:28; 1 Cor. 7:21–24). However, in 1 Timothy the stronger concern is not for the situation of the slave but for the missionary needs of the gospel and the public reputation of the faith. I have emphasized the words *so that* (Greek, *hina*) in 6:1 for a reason: this evangelistic and apologetic rationale for submission is found not only here but also in Titus 2, and each time the rationale begins with the word *hina*.

Titus 2:1–10 gives instructions ("sound doctrine") for Titus to pass on to older women and men, young women and men, and slaves. In each case they are to live sober and upright lives, according to the moral standards of that day and time. This instruction might be seen as a concern for holiness in the Christian home on general principles, but the "so that" clauses point us in a different direction. The motive here is, once again, missionary and apologetic. Titus is to have the older women encourage the young wives in the domestic virtues, including loving their husbands and children and being sensible, chaste, and submissive to their husbands. Why? "*So that* the word of God may not be brought into disrepute" (2:5). The young husbands should likewise control themselves and lead virtuous lives "*so that* an opponent may be put to shame, having nothing bad to say about us" (2:8). Finally a third group is addressed: slaves. They are to "give satisfaction in every way" and be in submission to their masters "*so that* they may adorn the teachings of God our Savior" (2:9–10). The religious motivation for the submission of socially inferior members within the public gaze of the secular community is hardly trivial. Putting opponents to shame and adorning the message of the gospel are obviously public matters of Christian mission and apologetics. The question could also be raised, are there not sound Christian reasons to do good works and live virtuous lives in this world? The answer to that is yes, and some of these general Christ-oriented reasons also appear in Titus 2:11–14. But the *manner* and *content* of these good works, for the socially inferior members of the church, focuses on submission to worldly authority. Once again, this is not a mutual submission (type II) but obedience to an external authority (type I submission). But why is this kind of submission being encouraged? The *hina*-clauses ("so that") point to a coherent and consistent reason: evangelical and apologetic concern for outsiders, who are closely observing members of this new religion. The reputation of the church and the honor of the Word of God are at stake here, and the submissive good behavior of Christians will help spread the gospel. While this chapter speaks to both women and men (but not to masters), the concern for submissive behavior is addressed only to those at the bottom end of the social hierarchy (older women/widows, wives, and slaves).

It is true that wives are commanded here to submit to their husbands as befits "sound doctrine." On a superficial reading, or one that ignored the larger social context of these letters, we might conclude that the moral doctrines enjoined in Titus 2 and 1 Timothy 6 are universal. Yet as we have already seen regarding the submission commands in 1 Peter, the ethics of submission in these letters are not for every time and place. They are specific to the situation of the churches in Crete and Ephesus, which were under the care of specific pastors (Timothy and Titus) in an age when Christianity was illegal, small, and easily slandered or persecuted. Christian concerns for evangelism, for cultural apologetics, and for living lives of good works and virtue as we enact our faith with fear and trembling (Phil. 2) are indeed universal concerns. But these normative principles of Christian discipleship do not lead to a universal call to *external submission* for either slaves or wives. That aspect of sound doctrine was local and temporary, limited to the social context of these letters.

These conclusions are based on a natural reading of the texts themselves. Yet not all agree with them. In an excursus on Titus 2:1–10 in his commentary on the Greek text of the Pastorals,

George Knight argues otherwise.[3] He believes that submission of women to men is part of the creation-order, something that is "intrinsically right" because both Christians and non-Christians "know in their conscience certain basics of right and wrong."[4] Being a twentieth-century Christian, Knight exempts the submission of slaves from these general and natural moral principles. But why? After all, Greek and Roman philosophers of the ancient world argued otherwise. They claimed that the submission of inferiors (including slaves) to their "natural" superiors (free men) is natural and a moral universal. Knight does claim that the interpersonal qualities asked of slaves are "right for any working condition,"[5] but this will hardly do. In this excursus, Knight tends to confuse virtue (a matter of one's stable character) with behavior. A virtue is a character trait, such as honesty or compassion, and should not be confused with a behavior, even though it may lead to certain kinds of action, such as speaking the truth. It is true enough that humility is a Christian virtue, but that virtue is not the same as acting in a humble way. In one of the most famous passages in the New Testament, Jesus calls "blessed" those who adopt Christian virtues such as humility and being merciful, along with those who "hunger and thirst for justice" (Matt. 5:4–7). Yes, these *virtues* can be universal. But the external submission (type I) called for in Titus 2 and 1 Timothy 6 is *not a virtue but a behavior*. And Knight fails to explain why virtuous Christian slaves and wives were specifically called to live out their Christian character in this particular manner. His only response is that "slavery itself is not being taught as a norm."[6] But this comment commits the fallacy of begging the question by assuming what Knight needs to prove—namely, that in the parallel cases of the exter-

3. George W. Knight, *Commentary on the Pastoral Epistles*, NIGTC (Grand Rapids: Eerdmans, 1992), 316–18.
     4. Ibid., 317–18.
     5. Ibid., 317.
     6. Ibid.

nal submission of wives and slaves, slavery is *not* being taught as a universal norm while man-centered leadership and wifely submission *are*.

Frankly, Knight is basing his view of Titus 2 not on the text itself but on other, better-known texts, in particular 1 Timothy 2:8–15. We now turn to this submission text to see if there is any exegetical basis for thinking that the submission of wives to husbands is a "creation-order" that is basic to the knowledge of right and wrong.

Adam and Eve at Ephesus: 1 Timothy 2:8–15

In my experience, 1 Timothy 2:8–15 is the passage most often cited by those who wish to perpetuate man-centered views of leadership (if they cite *any* biblical passage). A casual reading of the text does lead one to think that women are for all time banned from the public teaching of religion to men in church and that they must submit and learn in quiet instead. The rationale for this reading does indeed come from the story of creation in Genesis, and so appears to support the view that woman's submission is a creation-order, God's will for all families all the time. But this interpretation suffers from a large number of problems, making it in the end highly dubious. It typically ignores the literary and social context of the letter, and does not pay careful enough attention to the details of the text.[7] We can do better. Some of these details are particularly strange and deserve thoughtful consideration before we rush to conclude that in this passage at least we find the one-sided submission of women to be grounded in creation itself as the universal will of God.

I suggest that we pay careful attention once again to what the text itself says instead of to what we already believe it says.

7. For an academic investigation of the text in its literary and social context, with bibliography, see A. G. Padgett, "Wealthy Women at Ephesus: 1 Timothy 2:8–15 in Social Context," *Int* 41 (1987): 19–31.

Read carefully in its larger social and intellectual context, the teaching of Paul in this passage can be understood, but only with a bit of imagination and careful reflection. Perhaps if we read his argument from the bottom up (see also the next chapter on 1 Cor. 11) we will be able to generate a fresh approach to these words. By reading from the bottom up, one makes clear what is always true: the meaning of one verse is best known in the light of the larger text of which it is a part.

First Timothy 2:15 is one of the more difficult verses to interpret in the Pastoral Epistles. In a way, it is a shame we have to start with such a tough verse; on the other hand, when we see where Paul is going with his argument, when we get a grip on what this verse is about, we will have a key to understanding the whole of 2:8–15. The verse says, "Yet she will be saved through [the] childbirth, if they continue in faith and love and holiness, with self-control." One odd thing about the verse is the change in subject from singular ("she") to plural ("they"). When we understand this shift, we will know more about Adam and Eve at Ephesus! The "she" is best understood, in terms of good grammar, as a reference to the woman of the previous sentence, who is Eve. But "they" are the women of Ephesus, the ones who are addressed in 2:9–12. What is going on here? How can Eve be "saved through [the] childbirth"? To know the answer we need to glance just a bit at Jewish ways of interpreting the Bible (Old Testament) in the age of King Herod and the second temple.[8]

Adam and Eve at Ephesus

The Jews of Paul's day read their Bible very differently than modern scholars. They were imaginative and free in their interpretations, seeking to see the present situation in the larger frame

---

8. I found helpful many years back an article by Aída B. Spencer, "Eve at Ephesus," *JETS* 17 (1974): 215–22.

of biblical law and story. We call this kind of Jewish interpretation "midrash" or "midrashic." Among other texts, we find this imaginative and figurative reading of the Bible throughout the Jewish books, written in Greek by apostles and evangelists, that we now call the New Testament. Like the authors of the Dead Sea Scrolls, the Jewish intellectual Philo of Alexandria, or the authors of other sacred Jewish texts (like the Pseudepigrapha), the New Testament authors use figurative interpretation very often, playing on a single word or figure from the biblical text. This is a strange world for twenty-first-century people to enter into. Figurative interpretation does not fit our canons of scientific thinking or good exegesis, but it was the common way of understanding the Bible among the rabbis and scholars of that day.

Although he could base his arguments on a more literal sense of the text, we know that Paul, like the other New Testament authors, used figurative, midrashic interpretation of Scripture quite frequently. An example comes from 1 Corinthians 10:1–13. There Paul specifically uses the word *type* (*typos*) to describe the way the old biblical stories applied to the church in his day. As a result, for centuries this kind of imaginative, figurative reading of the Bible was called typology. Like other Jewish interpreters of his time, Paul held that the rock from which the Israelites drank in the desert (Exod. 17:6) actually followed them along in their journey to the promised land. But Paul adds two more elements to the story: (1) the rock gave them *spiritual* drink; and (2) the rock was the Messiah (1 Cor. 10:4). This kind of typological or midrashic interpretation should not be seen as strange or fanciful. It was considered at the time to be very learned and biblical and was taken quite seriously by biblically minded Jews.

Typology is not so much a genre or type of literature as it is a general approach to understanding the Bible. It is characteristic of midrash as a whole, in its many varieties and literary forms.

The assumption was that God is behind the sacred text, so it must have power and authority for today's world. In midrashic interpretation, there is no separation between application and interpretation, between past and present. Rather, the present situation was read back into the biblical text, and the biblical text came alive as part of the present situation. So Paul could interpret the temptation of Eve by the snake in 2 Corinthians 11:3–4 as the false teachers (snake) leading astray the thoughts of believers (Eve) from a pure devotion to Christ. Paul can interpret Christ as the "second Adam" and compare him to the first Adam (Rom. 5:12–21).

Finally, we know that Paul interpreted Genesis 3:15 in a typological (midrashic) way as well. Genesis 3:15 is God's curse upon the snake (who is nowhere called Satan or the devil in Genesis—that is a much later, figurative interpretation): "I will put hatred between you and the woman, between your seed [offspring] and hers; he [the "seed" of Eve] will strike your head, and you will strike his heel." The striking of the head of the snake is a mortal blow, while the seed or child of Eve will receive a lesser wound to the heel. In the age of Jesus and Paul, the snake was regularly seen as the enemy of God's people, Satan. One Jewish source also interprets the seed of Eve as "King Messiah." And Paul himself can write, in a midrashic echo of Genesis 3:15, "The God of peace will soon crush Satan under your feet" (Rom. 16:20).

With one exception (the genealogy in Luke 3:38), Adam and Eve appear in the New Testament as figures or types. We are now ready to return to our passage in 1 Timothy 2, which is no exception to this rule. Paul can change from *singular* (Eve) to *plural* (Ephesian women) in 2:15 because he is thinking of them together, in a typological way. (I will return to this point a little later, after looking at 2:12–13.) Eve and the Christian women of Ephesus will both be saved through the birth of Eve's "seed," who is *Christ*, as long as they (the women believers) continue in faith and love and holiness with self-control. After all, the "God of peace" will quickly crush the head of Satan, according to Romans 16:20, echoing a widely held Jewish expectation of the defeat of Satan (see, for example, Luke 10:18–19). The Prince of Peace may well appear also in Paul's midrashic reading of the story of Adam and Eve at 1 Timothy 2:15.

Some scholars have argued that the word *saved* here has a physical rather than a spiritual meaning. Certainly the verb *to save* can mean more than religious salvation, including being saved from illness or death. In this view, the women of Ephesus will be kept from bodily harm when they undergo childbirth, according to 2:15. But the spiritual sense of "being saved" is so very common in the New Testament—indeed, it is almost universal—that the burden of proof is on those who see this as a health-oriented salvation. What is more, the use of the word *through* (Greek, *dia*) makes this unlikely since, when "saved" (*sōzō*) is followed by "through" (*dia*), the salvation in question is always spiritual in nature in Paul's letters.[9] Also, the Christian virtues that follow this promise—faith, love, holiness, self-control—point toward circumstances of holy living in faith—that is, a spiritual salvation rather than bodily health or endurance through childbirth.

We have spent a long time on a single verse, and on Paul's typological reading of Adam and Eve, because this provides us with a sound introduction to the passage as a whole and an important key to interpretation. Adam and Eve appear at Ephe-

---

9. For example, see Titus 3:5; Romans 5:9; 1 Corinthians 15:2; and Ephesians 2:8; see also 1 Corinthians 3:15, where the salvation is spiritual, but "through" designates the circumstances: "as through fire." On the other hand, 1 Peter 3:20 gives a sense of physical salvation, speaking of the few lives that were "saved through water"—that is, kept safe (*sōzō*) through (*dia*) the waters of the flood. But in the Pastoral Epistles, "saved" is universally spiritual in its sense. In his influential article, Stan Porter rightly concludes that the passive verb in 2:15, *will be saved*, is "virtually guaranteed a salvific sense (the passive voice is probably a divine or theological passive, that is, God is the agent of salvation)" ("What Does It Mean to Be 'Saved by Childbirth' [1 Timothy 2:15]?" *JSNT* 49 [1993]: 94).

sus as *types*. The situation of the women at Ephesus is being interpreted in light of the Genesis story, and the story of Adam and Eve is being interpreted in light of the situation at Ephesus.

The Women of Ephesus

Having carefully considered 1 Timothy 2:15, we are now ready to move up a sentence or two. These verses provide another *rationale for submission*, this time with respect to women teaching men in church: "For Adam was formed first, and then Eve. Further, Adam was not deceived, but the woman, being deceived, fell into transgression" (2:13–14). Of all the things one might pick out of the story of Adam and Eve, the author finds two of relevance to his day: (1) the man was formed first, then the woman; and (2) the woman was deceived and thus fell into transgression of God's law. Now, we know from Genesis that Adam was also there, listening to the snake. He too was deceived and ate the fruit of the forbidden tree of moral knowledge (Gen. 3:6). Yet these points are ignored by our author, for one reason: they are irrelevant to the *typological* argument being made. The key points are the narrative parallel between Adam and Eve, on the one hand, and the issue between women and men at Ephesus, on the other. The most important parallel to this argument is not 1 Corinthians 14, as is sometimes claimed by commentators, but 2 Corinthians 11:3. As we noted before, in 2 Corinthians 11 Eve functions as a type of those who are being deceived by false teachers ("the snake"). She has the same function in this text.

It seems the false teachers, those opponents of the gospel that Paul and Timothy are taking on with this letter, were particularly successful among certain women (2 Tim. 3:1–9). The false teachers "make their way into houses [house-churches?] and capture weak-willed women" who are seeking to know the truth but are being led astray into sin (2 Tim. 3:6). The primitive church had no buildings of its own but met in the houses of believers. The house-churches we know of from the New Testament met in the homes of couples like Philemon and Apphia (Philem. 1–3), or in those owned by single women—very likely wealthy widows—like Lydia (Acts 16:14–15, 40) and Phoebe (Rom. 16:1–2). Since it was normal in the Roman world for tutors to charge for their services, the false teachers were probably making a bit of money from the people they were instructing. Paul in fact accuses them of greed, professing religion only to profit (1 Tim. 6:3–10). Of course we cannot be certain, and we have only hints from historical sources and the biblical text, but the scenario we just put together fits what evidence we have very nicely. We can be sure at least that these women were *wealthy* because of the way Paul talks about them in an earlier verse (2:9). The other parts of the background to this passage we piece together from what hints we can find.

Like Eve, these wealthy women were being deceived by the snake, that is, by Satan or at least Satan's minions, the false teachers. Because they listened to the "snake," these women had already fallen into sin. But what sin was this? Again, we cannot be sure, but it may well have had something to do with sex and the marriage bed. We know from this letter that younger widows were taking vows not to marry and were "going about from house [church?] to house," spreading gossip and "saying what they should not" so that "some of them have already strayed after Satan" (5:11–15). Religious aversion to marriage (and probably to sex in general), along with other aesthetic practices, was something the false teachers were pushing in the local church (4:3). This antimarriage teaching and practice must be the reason that Paul links up *childbirth* and *salvation* in 2:15. If these women will return to sound doctrine and living in faith, holiness, love, and modesty, then (1) they will be saved by the Prince of Peace, who (midrashically) is the "seed of Eve" who crushes the head of the snake/Satan (see Luke 10:18–19; Rom. 16:20; and many extrabiblical texts); *and also*

(2) they will be kept safe ("saved") through childbirth. This double reference to Eve and the Ephesian women is why verse 15 reads so oddly, and it explains the use of "the childbirth" in the context of salvation.[10]

We have been arguing for a midrashic, typological interpretation behind Paul's reference to Adam and Eve in 1 Timothy 2. Eve is pretty clearly a type of the women of Ephesus. But who is Adam? We have three clues to the contemporary man that the author may have had in mind. The first clue is the letter as a whole. It was written by Paul to support and instruct his co-worker and colleague in the gospel, Timothy. It builds up Timothy and promotes sound doctrine over against the social and intellectual leadership of the false teachers within the churches at Ephesus. The second clue is that "Adam" was "formed first" according to the text. And third, "Adam" was not deceived by the snake/false teachers. One does not have to be a famous detective to see that both Timothy and the sound doctrine or "gospel according to Paul" are the likely midrashic references hiding under the name of Adam here.[11] We saw earlier that it was particularly the young widows that were rejecting marriage.

10. In an influential article already cited, Stan Porter rejects this typological double reference, but his reasoning is unsound. While Porter is an excellent biblical scholar, he makes a *faux pas* by imposing modern Western notions of time and the arrow causation on an ancient text. Eve cannot be saved through the birth of the child (Messiah), he asserts, because her fate is in the past: "Since Eve's fortunes have already been determined, they are beyond any further expectation, so this solution is unlikely" ("What Does It Mean?," 92). Porter fails to take seriously the midrashic, typological mode of thinking in which *the modern sense of time plays no part*. And he does not notice that it is *the women* (plural) who continue in faith, love, and holiness, not Eve. So the "expectation" of holy living was upon them, not Eve, against the other objection by Porter. By the time these expectations come up, Paul has changed from singular (Eve) to plural (women of Ephesus). Thus both Porter's objections to the view presented in this chapter are themselves quite dubious.

11. In an interesting, well-researched recent article, Ken Waters demonstrates that "children" was a common metaphor of the day for the *virtues* or holy character that flowed from sound moral teaching ("Saved through Childbearing: Virtues as Children in 1 Timothy 2:8–15," *JBL* 123 [2004]: 703–35). Waters also argues for the term *allegory* as the correct technical term for the kind of interpretation going on in this passage.

Also, the *doctrines* of the false teachers were new, but the gospel according to Paul is one that he claims goes back to the earliest Christian sources (e.g., 1 Cor. 15:1–8). Indeed, the apostle can claim he learned it from the risen Christ himself (1 Cor. 15:8; Gal. 1:1, 11–12). Thus "Adam" (Timothy + Paul's instruction) is older and more mature, and not deceived by Satan's lies.

Having a sound understanding of the extended metaphorical meaning of Adam, Eve, and childbirth in 1 Timothy 2:13–15, we are now ready to look at what many supporters of man-centered leadership find to be the key to gender roles in the whole Bible, 2:11–12: "Let a woman learn in silence with all submissiveness. I do not permit a woman to teach or have authority over men, but she is to keep silent." The word *therefore* that starts verse 13 connects these commands to the story of Adam and Eve we have just reviewed. We have a few questions to ask of these sentences: Who are the women Paul is talking about? Is he speaking just about women at Ephesus in the time of Timothy, or to all women? To whom are these women supposed to be learning from in all submission? Let's take these questions one at a time.

The larger context of this passage makes it very likely that these commands are written to specific wealthy women (widows?) at Ephesus (see 2:8–10, often overlooked by those jumping right to vv. 11–12). It is *these women* who were causing dissension in the house-church meetings (as we will soon see) and spreading the doctrines of the false teachers. These women who were seeking to learn needed to "learn in silence," not teach or have authority over men, and be in all submission. Paul is thus not limiting the leadership and teaching/preaching roles of all women with these sentences. Such a universalizing reading ignores the larger context of these verses. Granted, those who hold on to man-centered leadership would insist that the appeal to creation in verses 13 through 15 makes these commands universal. But again, this is a misreading of the text

that ignores the figurative nature of this appeal. Paul's point is
not that by being formed first, Adam somehow has an inherent
superiority to Eve. After all, in the story of creation in Genesis
1–2 no such superiority is given to the man. Rather, the woman
solves the man's "not good" situation and is for this reason
the *appropriate partner* and *succor* of Adam (Gen. 2:18; not
"helper" or "help meet," as in KJV). The Genesis creation story
suggests not that Adam was "head" or authority over Eve but
that man needed woman (Eve) in order to be a whole human
being: "For this reason *a man* leaves his father and his mother
and clings to his wife, and they become one flesh" (Gen. 2:24).
If the so-called complementarian theology were really biblical,
we would expect that the wife clings to the husband; but that
is the opposite of what Genesis actually says! So despite first
appearances, the argument here is not that *priority leads to
authority over* or some kind of superior status for Adam/men.
As we have seen above, being made first in 1 Timothy 2:13 is
a metaphor for having older, sounder doctrine—being more
mature in the faith.

Genesis does speak of the authority of man over woman, but
not in chapter 2. Rather, as a result of sin and the fall, wives
will be "lorded over" or dominated by their husbands. Genesis
3:16—in the larger context of God's pronouncing judgment on
the snake, on the earth, and on Adam and Eve—speaks both of
domination and of bearing children (see 1 Tim. 2:15 again) in
pain or great labor: "I will greatly increase your labor in childbearing; in great labor [pain?] you shall bring forth children.
Still your desire will be for your husband, and he shall lord it
over you." Because of sin, the blissful relationship of oneness
described in Genesis 2 is turned on its head in Genesis 3. In a
world of sin, the wife will desire her husband, not vice versa;
and instead of being loved and adored as "one flesh," she will
be subject to male domination or being lorded over. Thus in
Genesis there simply is no authority given by God *in creation*

to the husband over the wife. Rather, both are created equally in the image of God (1:26–28), and both are "one flesh" in love and devotion, so that they can fulfill together the command to be fruitful and multiply. The so-called headship of the husband, understood as authority over, is a result of sin, not a creation-order. There is no biblical (or philosophical) basis for George Knight's claim, discussed earlier, that the submission of wives to husbands is a creation-grounded, "natural" moral truth.

Returning to 1 Timothy 2, to whom are these women of Ephesus supposed to submit? The context demands that they submit to "Adam," that is, to Timothy and Paul's sound doctrine. The idea that women are to be in submission to husbands or men is not at all the point. Rather, these women were *seeking to learn*. As we saw with a similar command in 1 Corinthians 14 (see the previous chapter), "silence" is a positive virtue for those who are hearing and learning the Word of God. It is not just that the women should shut up and be quiet; that's what we can easily feel about verse 11, but our feelings can lead us astray here. Rather, the point is that "a woman" should learn in silence and not take up authority over men by teaching in church. Such a woman learner is to be in complete submission *to sound doctrine* and *to the ministry of Timothy*, not to men in general.

Now we are ready to look at the start of the passage and read it as a whole. Paul actually begins by speaking to men, who were upset and showing their anger: "I desire that in every place [church?] the men should pray, lifting holy hands, without anger and argument" (2:8). Why were these men angry and arguing? Very likely it had to do with what Paul spends a lot more than one verse (to the men) talking about: the women of verses 9 through 15! Their spreading the doctrines and practices of the false teachers is probably the source of these arguments. "In every place" probably refers to the several house-churches of Ephesus.

Having started with men, Paul turns to the source of the trouble, the women: "Likewise the women should dress themselves in modesty and sensible, appropriate attire; not with braided hair, gold, pearls nor expensive clothes" (2:9). These are not generic phrases thrown out for fun; Paul has in mind specific women who were wealthy and were displaying that wealth in ways typical of the women of the Roman Empire. Their display of wealth may have been a subtle way of asserting their social authority, and some house-churches may have been meeting in the homes of these women. Notice already the presence of metaphor: the women are not to "dress" with costly attire but are to adorn themselves with the virtue of modesty. They should do good works, as befits women who are "preaching religion" (2:10). These women desired to have some authority in the local church, to learn more about their (new?) religion, and to spread the good news. But the source they turned to for instruction was false. Timothy had to correct them and teach them sound doctrine.

Conclusion

So does 1 Timothy 2:8–15 support a complementarian theology of gender roles? Not really, not when we take a closer look at the original text in its historical and literary context. Rather, this passage was written about certain wealthy women at Ephesus who were spreading false doctrines. Certainly a patriarchal interpretation of this passage has the great weight of a long tradition on its side and has many defenders today. But it just does not fit the facts very well.

In this chapter we have been looking at the submission passages that are usually used to support man-centered leadership. We have seen that a careful reading of the original text in context leads away from the usual patriarchal interpretation. Clues in the texts themselves suggest that these were not meant to be one-sided submission commands to wives or women believers, applicable for all time. In each case, the context and shape of these commands demonstrates their temporary nature. They were written during a time of persecution when church leaders were very concerned for the spread of the gospel and the reputation of the new religion in the larger community. They were written against false teachers and their doctrines, which in at least one place and time were very influential among some wealthy women believers who were seeking to learn more about their faith. They do not and should not provide solid footing for a man-centered theology of Christian leadership in the home.

For the last chapter or two our concern has been the original, historical meaning of specific texts. Our focus has been on what I earlier called the *conventional sense*. It is time now to look at the broader *canonical sense* and see what contemporary meaning these passages may have. Yet before we consider the contemporary sense of these texts, I would like to take a short detour to look at a rather complex passage in Paul's First Letter to the Corinthians concerning women and men in church.

5

Headship and Head-Coverings

1 Corinthians 11:2–16 from the Bottom Up

S o far in our study we have discovered the dominance of *mutual submission*, understood as taking up the role of a servant, in those passages in the New Testament that speak of humble, self-giving service. In discussing this biblical ethic, we looked briefly at 1 Corinthians 11:2–16. I have been fascinated by this passage, studying and writing about it for over twenty years. Even though this chapter is not central to the argument of the book, I cannot leave the topic of submission, headship, and gender roles without explaining the results of my long fascination with and investigation of this text.

While many ways of understanding this passage have developed over the millennia, the interpretation I prefer will require a fresh approach to the text. To this end, just to overcome years of misreading, I am going to ask you to read the passage from the bottom up.

Reading Passages from the Bottom Up

It often helps to look at the end of a difficult argument in order to understand it better. What is the author's main point? This should guide our interpretation of the whole passage. Paul's arguments are often quite difficult to follow. He was not a linear thinker. His prose is circular, even sinuous. The trick of looking at the end or main point of his argument works with many different passages. Consider Romans 8, for example, one of the most beloved chapters in the New Testament. It ends with a ringing declaration of the love of God. Nothing, not even death, can separate us from God's love in Christ. But the very next words are jarring in their change of direction. Paul writes that he is speaking the truth in Christ—not lying—about his great sorrow for his people, the Jews. What is the connection here? Many commentators have been puzzled by the "insertion" of chapters 9–11 in Paul's overall argument in Romans.

We have to remember that Paul's original text did not have verse or chapter divisions. In fact, paper was so expensive that scribes did not even leave spaces between words. So the "jump" from 8:39 to 9:1 must have been even more jarring to Paul's original readers. What is going on here? The answer is revealed only at the end of this long section, in what we call chapter 11. "Has God rejected his people?" Paul asks. No! "God has not rejected his people whom he foreknew" (11:2 NRSV). Aha! Now we see why, when speaking of the inseparable love of God for his people, Paul began to think of his own people, the Jews. Did God's love abandon them? Many of them stumbled and fell. Just as some Jews turned from God to idols, so in Paul's day some rejected the Messiah. God did not reject his people: they rejected him. We do not fully grasp the start of chapter 9 until we get to the end of chapter 11.

Another example of using the end of a line of thought in order to better understand the beginning comes from 1 Corinthians. In chapter 8, Paul begins his discussion of food sacrificed to idols. This is a long, complex, and cyclical argument from 8:1 to 11:1. For reasons that are not clear at first, Paul begins talking about knowledge. "All of us possess knowledge," he writes (8:1). What is going on here? How can we make sense of the beginning of this argument? We can get a good clue by looking at the end of the chapter, where he says that if eating food causes one of his sisters or brothers to fall, it would be better never to eat meat (8:13). Not everyone has the "knowledge" that some Corinthians admired, the knowledge that "an idol is nothing in the world" and "there is no God but one" (8:4). Because of their superior knowledge, some people in Corinth were eating meat that had been sacrificed to idols in pagan temples. Many commentators agree that the phrases in 8:4 come from the Corinthians themselves, probably from the letter they wrote to Paul (7:1). For this reason, the NRSV puts the phrases in quotation marks. These Corinthians "knew" that idols were nothing and could make no difference to the meat they ate. This practice, however, upset others who were against idol worship.

Looking at the end of Paul's argument, we can see why he began with a discussion of knowledge. We can see the point of his writing, "Knowledge puffs up, but love builds up" (8:1 NRSV). It becomes clear that 8:1–6 is not Paul's own theology but his description of the theology of his opponents, including even quotations of some of their own ideas. Paul then begins to refute their practice at 8:7: "But not everyone has this knowledge." So looking at the end of this chapter helps us rightly understand 8:1–6. In this case, looking at the end is not only helpful but also seems necessary for a proper interpretation of this passage.

Our task in this chapter is to offer a clear, attentive, and reasonable reading of 1 Corinthians 11:2–16. This is possible, I have found, only by knowing the end from the beginning of the text. To this end, not only will we be examining the passage from the bottom up, we will also take note of some background information, which is always helpful in understanding the text of any letter. Thus we begin to study this passage not at the beginning, but at the end.

Paul's Arguments from Nature and Consensus

First Corinthians 11:2–16 is the longest single passage in which Paul deals with issues relating to gender roles in the church. His concern does not arise from his own agenda but rather from a custom in the Corinthian church that he wishes to oppose. This much is clear from 11:16: "And if anyone is disposed to be argumentative, we have no such custom, nor do the churches of God." Paul was forced, time and again, to contend with various groups in Corinth and their aberrant theology and ethics. He corrects them patiently, like a good friend or parent, but also knows they are inclined to be argumentative. So in the end, he appeals to the practice of all the other churches. The rest of the churches have no such strange custom, no such demand upon believers in worship, which calls into question the local Corinthian custom. Paul has in mind here a particular custom and a particular group of Christians at Corinth who were insisting on this custom.

What was the custom? That is a question that has troubled commentators for thousands of years. The best clues to the nature of this custom come from verses 13 through 15, not from the earlier part of the passage. In verse 15 Paul writes, "For hair is given [by nature] to her instead of a covering." This phrase is important to Paul's argument. First of all, we discover that the custom has to do with proper dress in church, and in particular with covering the head in church. Paul argues that nature has given women long hair instead of a covering.[1] In verse 16 Paul gives an argument from what the rest of the churches do, that

1. See Padgett, "The Significance of ἀντί in 1 Corinthians 11:15."

is, he makes an appeal to consensus. In verses 13 through 15 he is giving an argument from *nature*, an appeal not unusual in the Greco-Roman world.

When we consider earlier verses, we discover that Paul mounts a total of four arguments against the Corinthian custom he is rejecting. We can only suppose that he found something in this custom offensive to his Christocentric thinking. His first argument has to do with the order of creation, that is, who came first, man or woman (vv. 8–10). Connected to this argument is Paul's assertion that "woman is the glory of man" (v. 7). The second argument is christological: in the Lord, differences between male and female have been overcome (vv. 11, 12). This is the part of the passage we have already discussed to some extent in this book. In his next two arguments, Paul moves from theology to common sense. "Judge for yourselves," he writes (v. 13). The third argument is from nature (vv. 13–15), while the final argument is from the consensus of the other churches (v. 16). We should pause to reflect on Paul's argument from nature before proceeding further up the passage.

Paul was familiar with arguments from nature. A native of Tarsus, Paul must have known of Stoic philosophy. Several Stoic philosophers hailed from Tarsus, in fact. The Stoics used to argue from nature—that is, from the way things are in a natural state. Paul's argument, then (which really turns on common sense), is a simple one: in a natural state, women have long hair, which nature has given them as a covering. This is part of his argument against the Corinthian custom.

Part of the custom in Corinth, therefore, seems to be that women should be covered in church. This is clear from the beginning of verse 13, when Paul asks the Corinthians to use their own common sense: "Judge for yourselves: is it proper for an uncovered woman to pray to God?" So our look at the end of the passage gives us the main issue between Paul and the Corinthians in the whole pericope. Paul's answer to the question he poses in verse 13 has been grossly misunderstood, however. In fact, this question may not be a question at all. Paul may have written a statement: "Judge for yourselves: it is proper for an uncovered woman to pray to God." This is a real possibility that should not be ignored (as it usually is). In the original text, there were no question marks and no real punctuation of any kind. So perhaps this was originally a statement, not a question. On the other hand, it is not impossible that this is in fact a question. In favor of taking this part of verse 13 as a question is the parallel verse in 10:15, where Paul writes, "I speak to reasonable people, judge for yourselves." This is followed by a question. However, if Paul is asking a question in verse 13, what is his answer?

This becomes clear in the next sentence. Even if we judge verse 13 to be a question—and it could well be a simple statement that it is proper for woman with an uncovered head to pray to God—the next two verses make no sense as anything other than a statement. They are usually forced into being another question, but in fact, they have never made any sense as such. The translation I recommend is this: "But nature herself has not taught you that if a man has long hair it is a shame while if a woman has long hair it is her glory; for hair is given to her instead of a covering."[2] If Paul did ask the question, "Is it proper for an uncovered woman to pray to God?" his answer is yes. He appeals to the natural state of things, in which men by nature grow long hair. There is no shame in a man with long hair. On the other hand, nature has given women long hair instead of (or "as the equivalent of") the coverings we often place on women's heads for cultural reasons (customs). Long hair is natural; it is not a "glory." Paul appeals past local human customs to the way God made us. As a statement, this sentence

2. I have been influenced in my reading of 1 Corinthians 11:2–16 by several older works, particularly Katherine Bushnell, *God's Word to Women*, 3rd ed. (Oakland, CA: private, 1930). Following W. F. Orr and J. A. Walther, *I Corinthians*, AB 32 (Garden City, NY: Doubleday, 1976), 261, I conclude that the Greek word *oude* ("neither") that starts this sentence was meant to be two words: *ou* ("not") and *de* ("but").

is a pretty good argument from nature against human customs. The force of Paul's words here has been blunted, however, by misunderstanding and mistranslation.

Translated as a question, this sentence would read, "Does not nature herself teach you that if a man wears long hair, it is a shame, but if a woman wears long hair, it is her glory?" The clear and sensible answer to this question is no. Nature teaches us no such thing! Yet the vast majority of commentators have forced Paul into the obviously false answer, "Yes, nature does teach that long hair on a man is shameful but long hair on a woman is glorious." When we interpret anyone's written text, we should use the principle of charity. Let us seek to understand the text in a way that makes sense of the author's words. Of course, at times authors do write rather silly things. My point is that tradition has done Paul a disservice in this case. The most sensible and reasonable way of reading Paul's words is as a statement.[3]

When you read Paul's words as a coherent whole, his argument is clear, and so is the custom that Paul is arguing against. This custom was based on social shame and social honor or "glory." It was shameful, at least in Corinth in those days, for a man to wear long hair (especially in church). It was also wrong for a woman to be uncovered (sometimes translated "unveiled") while praying. The custom Paul is opposing now becomes clear: on a woman long hair is beautiful, womanly, glorious; but on a man it is shameful. This is the "covering" custom that Paul is arguing against. The custom becomes clear only when we pay careful attention to the end of Paul's argument. We will study the social background of this custom in more detail as we approach the top of the passage, where Paul has more to say on this topic.

---

3. The most important translation of the Bible in Western history, the Latin Vulgate, does translate this as a statement, not a question. The Latin language, unlike the Greek, uses certain words or suffixes to indicate when a question is being asked. None of these are present in the Latin translation of 11:13–15. The Latin gets it right! I owe this point to my friend the Reverend Dr. Richard Sturch.

Paul's Christological Argument

Moving further up, then, the next verses (11–12) cover Paul's christological argument against the Corinthian custom: "Nevertheless, in the Lord, woman is not different from man nor man different from woman. For just as woman came from man, so man comes from woman, and all people come from God." The normal translation of this verse is unusually free of misunderstanding (for our passage, at least). Yet the power of what Paul is saying has been overlooked. The phrase "in the Lord" is not a minor one for Paul. On the contrary, everything in Paul's writing can be summed up under the concept of "being in Christ." Everything he says about justification, about holiness, about love, about the body of Christ, about spiritual gifts—everything can be summarized in the concept of "being in Christ" because this is the heart and soul of Paul's ethics and theology. Again and again, Paul corrects the Corinthians on the basis of his understanding of new life in Christ. This passage is no exception.

Paul often uses the term *nevertheless* to summarize the point he is making. Here, his main point is rather obvious, if we just pay attention to what he wrote. In the Lord, these differences of dress are of no importance. Social customs of dress, which distinguish male and female, should not inhibit a woman or a man from praying or prophesying in the worship of the Lord. After all, even if there was a temporal priority of man before woman in the creation story (Gen. 2), now men are born from women (their mothers), so that the balance is restored. This balance between male and female is key to Paul's entire argument, including the way he explains the Corinthian custom in 11:3–7. Because of this balance, Paul wants to affirm that "all people come from God" (v. 12). The Greek text just says "all come from God," and is usually translated "all things." Paul's argument, however, is not about things but about men and women. All people come from God, and the theological implication of this fact is that all people are created in the image of God (not just men, as 11:7 states).

That Paul would insist on gender balance in the image of God, and in the Lord, is nothing new. After all, Genesis specifically states that both women and men were created in the image of God (Gen. 1:26–27). As demonstrated earlier in this book, we find this same balance in 1 Corinthians 7 and Galatians 3. Paul was also quite willing to set aside accepted social divisions in the church. The division between Jew and Gentile was, if anything, even more central than that between man and woman for the Jewish theologians of Paul's day. Yet Paul sets aside this division in the Lord: "For there is no distinction between Jew and Greek; the same Lord is Lord of all and is generous to all who call on him" (Rom. 10:12 NRSV). The whole argument of the letter to the Galatians is that the distinguishing sign of circumcision, as a cultic marker, is overcome in the church (that is, in Christ). Paul's argument in this passage parallels that of Galatians. The distinguishing marks of short hair on men and head-coverings for women are of no consequence in the Lord or in church.

This view may seem rather "advanced" coming from a Jewish Christian of the first century. But we forget that Jesus accepted both women and men into his fellowship, and women alongside the men as his disciples. So Paul had a good role model in seeking gender balance in the Lord! He specifically writes, in 11:1, "Be imitators of me, as I am of Christ" (NRSV). The Jesus movement provided new, open opportunities for women. Scholars have only recently understood the extent of this new freedom for women in the apostolic age. Paul was in basic agreement with his Lord on this point—hardly a surprising development.

Paul's Argument from Creation and the Angels

The interpretation of Paul's words I am pressing for becomes even clearer in verse 10. Alas, here we have another case of a badly misunderstood and mistranslated sentence. Translators have inserted the words *symbol of* into this verse for a very long time. What Paul actually wrote is this: "For this reason a woman ought to have authority over her head, because of the angels." The NRSV, at least, has recognized this translation as an alternative in a footnote. As a matter of fact, this is simply the natural reading of the original Greek.

The word *authority* (*exousia*) is always, in Greek, the person's own authority, not someone else's. The phrase "have authority over" always means having power, freedom, or authority over something. Despite the common translation in English of "veil" or "symbol of authority," *exousia* never means—and indeed it simply cannot mean—having a symbol of someone else's authority on top of something. Recent commentators have recognized the power of this argument from good grammar and semantics but don't know what to do about it. I suggest we let Paul speak for himself. What Paul says is simple enough: women ought to have freedom to wear their hair however they want in church.

Does this seem so radical? Is it so odd and strange? Not at all! On the contrary, we have just seen that this point is exactly what Paul is arguing in verses 11 through 16. Once again, by reading from the bottom up, we have discovered the key to Paul's argument. Some Corinthians were insisting that women, when they prayed or prophesied, wear a kind of covering over their head. They also thought it shameful for a man to have long hair. Paul is arguing against them, basing his argument on gender balance in Christ, on what is natural, and on consensus among other churches. Women ought to have the freedom to wear their hair as they see fit in the worship service. After all, nature has given women long hair instead of a covering; they don't need another one.

Paul gives two reasons that women ought to have freedom over their heads. The first part of verse 10, "for this reason," points us back to the sentences just prior to this verse. Since we are reading from the bottom up, we will come to them next. But Paul's secondary reason is very obscure: "because of the angels." What on earth do angels have to do with women's covering? This brief reference, almost an aside, is so short and strange that we may never know what Paul meant by these words. Most of the time in the Bible, the Greek word *angelos* means a heavenly messenger, a supernatural being. An example of this is Galatians 1:8, in which "an angel from heaven" refers to a supernatural being. But on a few occasions, the word can mean a human being who is a messenger, as, for example, in Galatians 4:14: "You received me as a messenger [*angelos*] of God, as Christ Jesus." Since both Paul and Jesus are human beings, the messenger (*angelos*) in this case refers to a human being, not an angel.

If we apply this meaning of *angelos* as a human messenger of the gospel to 1 Corinthians 11:10, then we might translate this phrase "because of the messengers." Women did have important roles in spreading the gospel in the early church. A good example is Priscilla, who, along with her husband, Aquila, labored side by side in the gospel with Paul, even in Corinth (Acts 18). Should not such a "messenger" have the freedom to wear her hair however she wishes in church? If this interpretation is correct, then "because of the messengers [of the gospel]" has about the same force as the argument from other churches in verse 16. It is a very cryptic remark about church and custom that he develops more fully later in the passage.

But suppose that this reading is rejected. As some scholars have pointed out, the word *angel* almost always means a supernatural being in Paul's letters—but not always! It is also true that in 1–2 Corinthians the word *angel* always (outside of v. 10) means a supernatural being. What could Paul mean by the phrase "because of the angels" if he was referring to a supernatural being? We can make some reasonable assumptions that will guide us in finding a good interpretation. Notice that this phrase is short and is left without any fuller explanation. We can assume that the meaning of this phrase would have been well known both to the Corinthian Christians and to Paul. Where can we look for teachings about angels that both the Corinthians and Paul had in common, and that would provide background to understanding his comment? One source is the Bible—that is, the Hebrew Bible or Old Testament. Another possible source is the letter that the Corinthians wrote to Paul. A third source might be Paul's own teachings, the "traditions" that he handed down to his disciples (11:2). A final source could be the deeds and teachings of Jesus, which we can assume were also handed down in oral form. One of these is surely the source of this teaching, because Paul simply mentions it in passing.

Unfortunately, we do not possess the letter from the Corinthians to Paul. If we did, it would shed great light on our understanding of early Christianity and of Paul's letter. What we do have are Paul's own letters, which give no indication of any teaching about angels in the areas of sex, gender, or family. There is, however, one passage from the Greek Old Testament (Septuagint) that mentions angels, women, and sex. This strange verse is Genesis 6:2: "The sons of God saw that they were fair; and they took wives for themselves of all that they chose" (NRSV). The Septuagint has "angels" instead of "sons of God." On the basis of this verse, Tertullian argued that women should have a veil over their heads because angels may lust after them.[4] Frankly, despite my respect for Tertullian, this interpretation seems absurd. In any case, Paul did not write that women should have a veil over their heads but that women should have freedom over their heads. There is not much help in the Old Testament for understanding Paul's reference to angels in 1 Corinthians 11.

---

4. Tertullian, *De virginibus velandis* 7 (ANF 4:32).

In the sayings of Jesus, however, we may find some help. Paul has already referred to the sayings of Jesus in the context of sexual ethics in this letter. In chapter 7, he refers to Jesus' teachings on divorce: "To the married I give this charge—not I, but the Lord" (7:10). We have already seen too that in 11:11 Paul will refer to life "in the Lord." Would it be so strange, then, for him to refer in 11:10 to a saying of Jesus?

The saying of Jesus to which Paul may be referring in 1 Corinthians 11:10 is about marriage in the resurrection. In response to the questioning of some Sadducees, Jesus affirms that there will be no marriage in the resurrection. Rather, we shall be "like the angels in heaven" (Mark 12:25). This saying is found in two other Gospels—Matthew 22:30 and Luke 20:36—and may well have been known to the Corinthians. Of the various sources we have to help us understand "because of the angels," this saying of Jesus provides us with the most likely background. Many scholars agree that some of the Corinthians, who sought after spiritual knowledge, already considered themselves "spiritual" people (1 Cor. 1:5; 3:1; 14:37). They had in a spiritual sense already entered into the kingdom of God (4:8). They had already become "like the angels," and things of the flesh were of no consequence to them. If this insight into Corinthian theology is correct, then we can see the force of Paul's argument. If the Corinthians had already become "like the angels," then Paul was saying that gender distinctions were of no importance. This is where the saying "of the Lord" comes in: Jesus teaches that in the resurrection, sexuality as we know it will be no more. So sexual distinctions, like head-coverings, should, in the Lord, be of no importance. Therefore, "because of the angels" women should not have to cover themselves when men do not. They should have freedom (to cover or not to cover) over their heads. This interpretation seems to make the most sense of the text, if one insists on viewing "angels" here as supernatural beings.

The more I think about "because of the angels," the more convinced I am that the earlier theory is more probable—namely, that "angels" in verse 10 refers to women who were messengers of God. The argument anticipates the one found later in verse 16, and it makes good sense in the overall context of Paul's argument. On the whole, which of these two readings is correct is difficult to say with certainty. I tend to favor the first interpretation, but the second one may be correct.

We can now press on to the first reason Paul gives that women ought to have control over their own heads. Verse 10 begins, you will remember, with the phrase "for this reason." This short phrase points us back to his earlier argument. To grasp the structure of the argument at this point, we need to look back to verse 7. Paul's argument has a familiar structure that is often found in the Bible, known by scholars as a "chiasm." A chiasm is a passage that generally has the structure A, B, B′, A′. In this kind of structure, there is a movement in to a central point, and then a parallel movement back out from the center, touching upon the same themes in a new way. Paul's argument in verses 7 through 10 has the following structure:

A Man *ought* not to have his *head* covered
   B   because he is in the image and *glory* of God.
   B′ But the woman is the *glory* of man [explication].
A′ For this reason she *ought* to have freedom over her *head*.

To better understand this argument and its structure, we need to look at verses 7 through 10 in their entirety.

> [7]For, on the one hand, a man ought not to have his head covered because he is the image and glory of God; but on the other hand, woman is the glory of man. [8]For man was not made from woman, but woman from man; [9]furthermore, man was not made because of woman but woman because of man. [10]For this reason, a woman ought to have freedom over her head.

Paul's reason for arguing that women in Corinth ought to have freedom or control over their heads is straightforward: "woman is the glory of man" (v. 7b). Some commentators have twisted Paul's word *glory* and tried to make it mean "reflection" (see the NRSV). Their arguments are more amusing than edifying, however, and have little value as careful exegesis. Paul's word here just means "glory" and cannot be reduced to some lesser status. If we pay attention to Paul's own words, then he must be saying something positive about women. After all, this is the reason that Corinthian women ought to have freedom over their own bodies.

In a long parenthesis in his chiastic argument, Paul appeals to the stories of Genesis 1–2. Man alone was "not good" (Gen. 2:18). This is in fact the first not-good thing in the Bible, all other things being good or even "very good." The woman was created out of man as the crowning glory of the creation story and as the succor ("help meet" in the KJV) of the male. As we have already seen in this book, the Hebrew word for "helper" does not indicate help from an inferior but from a superior (or equal) person. The noun is often used of God, for example. So "helper" in English does not convey the force of the Hebrew noun. The English word *succor* is better because it indicates that Eve is an equal partner for Adam (in the Hebrew text), not just a servant or gardener. Notice, for example, that the *man* leaves his family and *clings to the woman* (Gen. 2:24). It is true that woman is created out of the male. But this is her glory, according to Paul, not an indication of inferior status. After all, Adam is created out of the dust, but is hardly inferior to dirt! No, the story tends to go from the lesser to the more glorious in Genesis 1–2. Paul understood this point, and so wrote that "woman is the glory of man . . . because woman was created out of man" (1 Cor. 11:7–8).

Paul immediately shifts from this argument from creation, however, to argue that "in the Lord" such distinctions have been overcome (vv. 11–12). Paul is more comfortable with gender balance (see, for example, 1 Cor. 7 and Gal. 3) than with one sex being more glorious than the other.

But what did Paul mean when he wrote, "For, on the one hand, a man ought not to have his head covered because he is the image and glory of God"? (v. 7a). Was Paul teaching that only the male is in the image and glory of God? Paying attention to the whole passage, we discover that this sentence is not Paul's own view but his description of a Corinthian view. Paul in fact rejects the idea that the male alone was "heavenly" or in the image and glory of God. Such theology will later make its way into some gnostic-influenced writings in the ancient world.[5] Paul's opponents in 1 Corinthians 11:2–16 may have been early followers of some concepts that, a century later, become part of gnostic thought.[6] In any case, the point of Paul's argument is to *refute* the view that the male alone was fit to inherit the kingdom of God. This idea is the primary theological root of the Corinthian custom and was a theological concept that troubled Paul enough for him to include hairstyle among the topics of this letter.

Paul's Perspective on Corinthian Head-Covering

We now have the key that will unlock the mysteries of 11:4–7a. Paul uses strange language here—so strange that some modern scholars have argued that he could not have written it and that these verses must have been inserted into the biblical text later, by another person. However, when we understand that these

5. See, for example, the *Gospel of Thomas*, saying 114, or the *Acts of Paul and Thecla*, par. 25 and 40; both apocryphal works can be found in W. Schneemelcher, ed., *New Testament Apocrypha*, 2 vols. (Louisville: Westminster John Knox, 1991). See also Kurt Rudolph, *Gnosis: The Nature and History of Gnosticism*, trans. Robert McLachlan Wilson (San Francisco: Harper & Row, 1983), 257, 270–72.

6. That Paul's opponents were influenced by theology that would later develop into gnosticism (with many other factors included) is widely believed by many modern commentators.

sentences are describing the Corinthian situation, we see his language in a whole new light.[7] For one thing, this insight helps to explains his strange use of vague Greek words to describe the covering custom of the Corinthians.

So Paul's description of their customs and theology is *not* neutral. On the contrary, he describes their views in such a way as implicitly to criticize them. The Corinthians held that when women prayed or prophesied in the church, they should wear a kind of shawl that they pulled up over the backs of their heads. It was common to insist in Roman culture that those who participate in the worship of the gods cover their heads in this way when they bring an offering.[8] This covering, then, was not for normal attendance at church, but just for those women who were leading church services.

According to the Corinthians, the men, on the other hand, should wear their hair short when they attend church, especially when they are church leaders. Long hair on men was seen as barbaric in Greek and Roman culture during this period. In particular, male church leaders should come to worship with short hair. Paul correctly describes this custom in terms of cultural control, especially *shame*. He takes great pains to create a parallel description of this Corinthian custom for men and women, in keeping with the gender balance he will insist on. By describing this custom in a way that is parallel for women and men, Paul sets up his later rejection of it: "Any man who prays or prophesies with something coming down from his head shames his head. But any woman who prays or prophesies with something coming down from her head shames her head" (vv. 4–5). Paul uses the same terms in Greek for the covering of male and female for a simple purpose: the words were vague enough

7. See the rather neglected article by Samuel T. Lowrie, "I Corinthians XI and the Ordination of Women as Ruling Elders," *PTR* 19 (1921): 113–30.

8. See David W. J. Gill, "The Importance of Roman Portraiture for Head Coverings in 1 Corinthians 11:2–16," *TynBul* 41 (1990): 245–60.

to include both long hair on men and the shawl-like covering for women in order to bring out the parallel situation for both women and men. His ultimate purpose is to reject the custom he is describing. Hairstyle for men played a part in the Corinthian custom, but the key problem no doubt has to do with the women, since he spends much more time on them. His description continues: "it is the same as if she were shaved" (v. 5b). Here we see the Corinthian idea (hardly found only in Corinth!) that long hair is glorious on a woman. Paul specifically rejects this cultural viewpoint later in the passage (v. 15). Not wearing the proper covering over her head while leading a church service is just as culturally bad, just as shameful, as having her glorious, long hair cut off—so the Corinthians believed.

Paul then goes on to exaggerate their viewpoint for the purpose of making fun of it: "For if a woman will not cover herself, she should cut off her hair; but if it is shameful for a woman to cut off her hair, let her cover it" (v. 6). This sentence is similar to one in Galatians, in which the custom of circumcision for Gentile men who converted to Christianity is refuted. In 5:12 Paul writes, "I wish those who unsettle you would castrate themselves!" (NRSV). If Paul's opponents at Galatia are so in favor of circumcision, he chides, why not go all the way? But of course, Paul does not really want them to be castrated. Likewise, he does not want the Corinthian women to have their hair cut off. In each instance he uses sarcastic exaggeration to poke fun at a custom he is opposing. Paul in fact was seeking to liberate the church from both circumcision and head-covering.

This interpretation does leave us with a good question: if it was common in Roman culture to cover one's head during the worship of the gods, why did the men not have to cover their heads? The Corinthian answer was straightforward: the male (alone) is in the image and glory of God (1 Cor. 11:7a), so he does not need to cover his head in the presence of God the way a woman does. Paul's counterargument is that, on the other hand, woman is the glory of man. As such, she should have freedom over her head, that is, freedom to wear her hair as she sees fit when engaging in the worship of God alongside the men.

Paul's Theology and Corinthian Customs

Reading from the bottom up, we are left to examine the first two verses. Paul begins this passage, "I praise you because you remember me in everything and maintain the traditions even as I have delivered them to you. And I want you to know that the head of every man is Christ, the head of woman is man, and the head of Christ is God" (11:2–3). There are several remaining puzzles in this beginning to our passage. We will discover that, having read the passage backward, we are in a good position to understand Paul's words.

Why does Paul commend the Corinthians here? He does so nowhere else in this letter. The reason, probably, is that they were boasting of holding on to the theology ("traditions") that Paul had taught them. Never mind that they grossly misunderstand and abuse it! Paul, tongue in cheek, praises them at this point. The "praise" that he gives them in this verse, however, only sets up the "I do not praise you" of verse 17 in the next passage.

The Corinthians claimed that they were only following the teachings Paul had handed on to them. And what were these teachings? Verse 3 tells us: God is the "head" of Christ, Christ is the "head" of man, and man is the "head" of woman. The word *head* in Greek, when not used to refer to the thing on top of our necks, has a variety of metaphorical meanings. We took note of this earlier, along with the idea that the metaphorical meanings can be summarized under the notion of being first in some way.[9] Sometimes being first or uppermost might mean having a kind of authority. At other times being first might mean being at the

---

9. See Perriman, "The Head of a Woman." Scholars have rightly rejected arguments that the metaphorical use of "head" in Greek never means authority or source.

start or being a source. These multiple meanings, then, provide a theological foundation for the Corinthian custom.

Paul begins to break up their hierarchy even in the way he describes it. This three-part "headship" sentence is not written in descending order. Paul purposefully broke up the top-down thinking of his opponents, even in his description of their ideas. He begins his description with "I want you to know." This phrase (and its equivalent, "I don't want you to be ignorant") was a cliché in Greek letter-writing in Paul's time. He uses it in an ironic way throughout 1 Corinthians 10–12. In all three of these chapters, Paul in fact wants to correct the Corinthians in an area they *thought* they already knew better than he did! In 1 Corinthians 10:1 he reminds them of the story of Moses, but of course they already knew such elementary things (cf. 1 Cor. 4:10). In 12:1 he corrects them in the area of spiritual gifts, again a place where they were already "experts" (cf. 1 Cor. 1:5). Likewise, here in 11:3 the phrase "I want you to know" is used in an ironic manner. In Paul's description he is simply repeating back to the Corinthians their own views. This sets up his correction of their theology in 11:7b–16.

Just what was the meaning of the three-part headship formula? The sense of "head" in 11:2–16 is that of being first in time or of being the origin. The idea of authority is foreign to 11:3. By reading from the bottom up, we already know that Paul will talk about who comes first in time, man or woman. So we have a good clue as to the meaning of "head" in this verse. Paul must have taught the Corinthians that Christ came from God (the origin of Christ is God). Likewise, Paul must have taught them that Christ is the origin ("head") of the church; but the Corinthians had restricted the "headship" of Christ to the male alone ("the head of man is Christ"; cf. v. 7a). Finally, Paul and the Bible taught that woman was created out of man ("the head of woman is man"). The theology of verse 3 was used as the basis for the head-covering custom of verses 4–6.

By reading this passage from the bottom up and paying attention to Paul's own words, we have discovered at last a reasonable interpretation of 11:2–16. We have in fact discovered that this passage has, in general, the same structure as 1 Corinthians 8. In both passages we find allusions to, perhaps even direct quotations from, the Corinthian letter to Paul. In both passages Paul describes the theology and custom of the Corinthians before he goes on to reject it. But how do we know for certain that 8:1–6 and 11:3–7a reflect Corinthian theology and practice rather than Paul's own? Four signs point in this direction.

1. Paul immediately rejects this theology and practice in the larger context of his argument.
2. The phrases that appear to come from the Corinthian letter give theological support to the practice Paul is rejecting.
3. The phrases that appear to come from the Corinthian letter would be strange coming from Paul. They are un-Pauline in their language and thought.
4. This theology and practice fit with what we know (from other places) about Paul's opponents in Corinth, or more generally, his correspondents.

Based on all four of these signs, 11:3–7a turns out to be Corinthian, not Pauline. Paul taught that Christ was the head of the church, not head of the male. Paul taught that all people were from God, not that the male alone was in the image and glory of God. Paul consistently rejected local customs (like hairstyles in worship) that inhibited liberty in Christ, *unless* the gospel itself was somehow at stake.

Conclusion

By reading from the bottom up, we have opened a new space to look again at a difficult passage. Careful attention to Paul's own words and to the type of letter he wrote (that is, one that cites the views of his opponents) has helped us understand this passage in its original setting. We can grasp the logic of Paul's argument in 11:2–16 in a way that makes sense of each part of the passage, of the passage as a whole, and of its place in the letter. What more can we ask of a proposed interpretation? I conclude, therefore, that by reading from the bottom up we have discovered the most likely interpretation of this passage. This reading is much more in keeping with everything we know about Paul, his theology, his common practice, and his ethical thinking. We discover, in fact, that Paul was seeking to give greater liberty to men and women in Christ. Paul was only interested in hairstyles because the Corinthian custom he was rejecting was based on aberrant theology. Paul rejected the notion that the male alone is in the image and glory of God, insisting that woman was the glory of man and as such ought to have freedom over her head.

Having examined every important passage on submission in the New Testament, we are ready to turn from consideration of the conventional sense of passages concerning submission to their contemporary meaning.

6

Submission Today

Hunger and Thirst for Justice

An episode of *The West Wing* opens with the president and first lady returning from church on a Sunday morning.[1] The homily that day was from Ephesians 5. The two have a friendly and witty debate about the implications of the passage for marriage today. President Bartlett insists that both the priest and his wife missed the main point: it is not about who gets the say-so in the home; rather, it is about submitting ourselves one to another in the fear of Christ.

What Aaron Sorkin put in the mouth of the fictional president in this much-lauded television series is the main point of our book. Despite their initial appearance, the submission passages in the New Testament are not really about those who are weak always giving in to those in power. This reading has, of course, been all too common in church history, especially since the union of church and state under Constantine. Such an

1. "War Games," teleplay by Aaron Sorkin (Warner Brothers Television; first aired November 7, 2001).

approach isolates a few solitary passages and ignores the rest of the New Testament. Most important, it ignores the model and teachings of Jesus Christ. In the end it is not a fully *Christian* reading of the submission ethics of the New Testament.

Our approach in this book has been to carefully examine the texts on submission, but always in the light of Christ and the gospel. We have argued that this is a truly evangelical approach to biblical interpretation. Putting Jesus at the center of our understanding of Scripture on this topic means that the teaching of Jesus on servant leadership and his enacted parable of washing the disciples' feet give us essential clues about how to live out the command to submit to each other today. Jesus' ethic implies that those in power should give of themselves to their sisters and brothers, to "the least of these." This call to radical discipleship, to follow Jesus in the way of the cross, is a very different notion of submission from that which was typical of the Roman Empire. Political submission is indeed a kind of forced, external act. We have called this type I submission. But Christian submission is a voluntary self-giving. It does not attack us where we are already weak or wounded, but calls forth the gifts of God in those places where the Holy Spirit's grace is at work in our lives, that we might in turn give to our neighbors.[2]

At the beginning of this study we argued that evangelical biblical ethics can never be satisfied with the study of an isolated verse. Of course the study of the original or *conventional* sense of the text is decisive for understanding Scripture; but the meaning of any one passage is not authoritative on its own. Only the whole of Scripture gives us the rich, complex teachings on salvation and discipleship that God has seen fit to give to the church. Only the whole of Scripture is the Word of God. Each passage should be

2. Sarah Coakley comes to a similar conclusion through a different route. She is in dialogue with feminist thought, philosophy in general, the history of doctrine, and contemplative prayer in her significant work *Powers and Submissions* (Oxford: Blackwell, 2002).

studied in the light of the whole Bible, with Jesus himself, the living Word, providing the interpretive key to the whole. I have called this the *canonical* sense of Scripture. We seek this canonical sense as a community of faith; when we do, we are on much firmer ground in claiming to be biblical people. Against too many church leaders in the evangelical movement, we must resist reductionist prooftexting in our efforts to understand the full will of God. Only the whole of Scripture, read as a whole, is a firm foundation for the reform of the church and the life of daily discipleship. Thus the canonical sense is essential in seeking to apply biblical teachings to our lives today. Our goal in this final chapter, in keeping with our understanding of moving from the canonical to the contemporary sense, is to ask what these submission passages might mean for us today, in the light of Scripture as a whole.

Power, Submission, and Self-Love

We have discovered in our study of key passages that mutual submission and servant leadership are almost the same thing. Both imply that we take up the role of a servant for a period of time and in a specific context. The only difference is that servant leadership is an ethic for leaders, while mutual submission applies to everyone in the body of Christ. This kind of mutual submission is not permanent and does not imply a hierarchy; rather, it is flexible, dynamic, and based on self-giving love. Servant leadership is an ethic of roles in which the one taking up the role of a servant is in fact a leader of some kind. The important point for the use of power in Christian relationships is this: those in power use that gift to empower others, especially those who are weak. This is what Jesus commands, what he demonstrated in his own ministry, and what Christian submission is about when rightly understood.

This taking up of a temporary role at a specific time and within a specific community is just one concrete way in which believers fulfill the command of Christ to love one another. The greatest command of all, of course, is to love the Lord our God. The active giving of oneself is connected to this greatest of all commandments. God's love flows through us, empowering us also to give, in service to our neighbors. But the love God commands is never self-destructive. God dies on the cross so that we don't have to. On the contrary, the second greatest commandment links love of others with a proper self-love: love your neighbor as you love yourself (Lev. 19:18; Matt. 22:39).

Unfortunately, the church has not grasped these truths very firmly for much of its history. The commands to submit and to love the neighbor have been abused by those in power to keep down the oppressed and the poor. There is overwhelming evidence—both today and in the history of the church—that biblical phrases like "submit to your husbands" or "submit to your masters" have been quoted in a way that condones and perpetuates wife abuse or slavery. Such teachings perpetuate injustice, violence, and oppression. These things are sin and evil, not the will of God. Sadly, this so-called biblical mandate often comes from the very ones that the beaten, downtrodden faithful look to for spiritual guidance: their priests or pastors.

In a genuine biblical ethics, self-love and love of neighbor balance each other, and both are grounded in the greater love of God. Yet here a problem of application arises. True love cannot decide between loving actions based on love alone. In the balance between love of self and love of others, *love needs to be guided by justice.*

Submission and the Hunger for Justice

A canonical overview of ethics will always find a strong biblical witness to justice. Perhaps the prophets of the Old Testament provide the best-known examples, but the cry for justice is common throughout the whole of the Christian Bible. Who can forget the famous words of the prophet Amos, "Let justice roll down like waters, and righteousness like an everflowing stream" (5:24 NRSV)? Isaiah goes so far as to identify justice as an attribute of God: "For the LORD is a God of justice; blessed are those who long for him" (30:18). The God of Scripture is indeed a God of love and mercy; but this is balanced by the Lord being a God of justice.

Jesus may have had the words of the prophet Isaiah in mind when he pronounced this blessing in the Sermon on the Mount: "Blessed are they who hunger and thirst after justice, for they shall be filled" (Matt. 5:6). The Greek term *dikaiosunē* used here can be translated as "righteousness," but it can also have the sense of "justice" or "uprightness." In the context of the Beatitudes, we can see it is the poor, hungry, and thirsty—that is, the "meek" or lowly persons—who are hungering for God's justice to be done. This context suggests that *dikaiosunē* should be translated "justice," thus avoiding the sense of "personal righteousness." The blessing is pronounced on those on the margins of society who are hungry and thirsty for God's justice. They are seeking for God's reign and realm to come on the earth, for God's will to be done here and now.[3] They will be satisfied with good things.

The hunger for justice is strong in any situation of oppression and abuse. This is just as true in our day as it was in the time of Amos or Jesus of Nazareth. Yes, mutual submission is an important aspect of biblical ethics. But the application of this self-giving love in today's world must balance concerns for both love and justice. Such a biblically grounded evangelical ethic will of course pay careful attention to the context of application. We should always remember that Jesus' call to care for "the least of these" comes to those who are leaders, who want to be "great in God's kingdom." It is where one is strong that God calls us to give to the needy and oppressed. It is where the Holy Spirit

3. Donald A. Hagner, *Matthew 1–13*, WBC (Dallas: Word, 1993), 93.

gifts us that we are enabled by God to give of ourselves to others. The Christian ethic must never be used to justify a situation of abuse and oppression. The command to submit should be spoken first of all to those in power, and modeled foremost by those who—like Jesus when he washed the disciples' feet—are fully aware of their authority.

To apply a fully orbed canonical ethic to our world today takes wisdom. Of all the virtues, prudence or wisdom has long been considered the most important, for wisdom guides the believer and the church in understanding God's will for a specific situation. The contemporary sense of Scripture must be grasped by reason and applied by wisdom, both of them being gifts of the Holy Spirit. This is no doubt why James begins his wisdom letter like this: "If any of you is lacking in wisdom, ask God, who gives to all ungrudgingly, and it will be given to you" (1:5). Knowing the biblical text is very important, of course, but so is a wise soul illuminated by God's grace. All these are important keys to applying the biblical ethic of love and justice today.

The Wisdom of Submission in Marriage

A friend of mine jokingly gives the following advice to husbands: "Submit early; submit often."[4] The man-centered ethics of complementarity would have us believe that submission does not apply to husbands. The man is in charge at home. Those who hold this position think that male leaders in the home and the church will lead with love, to be sure, but that a man is always at the top of the hierarchy. Women should submit to some man or other, and cannot have authority unless they are under a proper "male spiritual head."

We have discovered that this ethic is in fact unbiblical. It can be found in a verse or two, certainly, but it is not what the Bible as a

---

4. This is known as "Rolnick's Dictum"—at least this is what my friend Phil Rolnick calls it.

whole tells us about the way Christians should treat each other. Rather, servant leadership simply is mutual submission in action when one is a leader. Christ shows us the way by himself submitting to us. Husbands and wives alike are called to this balanced self-giving out of reverence for Christ and love for one another.

In practice the balanced give-and-take of mutual submission will require wisdom. No specific behavior or concrete rule will fit every situation. Instead, Christians who are wives and husbands should live, talk, and work together to do what is best for the family as a whole. Different people will have different strengths, and so will take the lead in different ways. No one person is always in charge. Part of the joy of being married is working out these things by talking together, trying things out, and seeking God's will in the day-to-day activities of life. It is always a matter of prayer. It is not really a matter of power *over* someone. That's what love really means in practice.

Just as God is always both merciful and just, so both love and justice will always be part of a balanced Christian approach to mutual submission. Taking up the role of a servant will be temporary, and can never be an excuse for ignoring the demands of justice and righteousness. This applies both to me and to those I seek to serve. Servant leadership in Christ should never be a form of oppression.

The argument of our final chapter concerns the contemporary meaning of the submission passages in the New Testament. Looking at the Bible as a whole, with Christ at the center, we can see that submission can never be an isolated ethic. The command to submit to one another is part of a much larger ethic, one grounded in the love of God. This ethic uses wisdom to balance love of self, love for the neighbor, and the quest for justice. It is always within this larger vision of love and justice that the Spirit-filled community of believers follows the Master's example of submission to one another.

Bibliography

Abraham, William J. *The Coming Great Revival: Recovering the Full Evangelical Tradition*. New York: Harper & Row, 1984.

Agosto, Ephrain. *Servant Leadership: Jesus and Paul*. St. Louis: Chalice, 2005.

Ante-Nicene Fathers. Edited by Alexander Roberts and James Donaldson. 10 vols. Peabody, MA: Hendrickson, 1994.

Applbaum, Arthur I. *Ethics for Adversaries: The Morality of Roles in Public and Professional Life*. Princeton: Princeton University Press, 1999.

Aristotle. *The Complete Works of Aristotle*. Edited by J. Barnes. 2 vols. Princeton: Princeton University Press, 1984.

Balch, David L. *Let Wives Be Submissive: The Domestic Code in I Peter*. Chino, CA: Scholars Press, 1981.

Barclay, John. *Obeying the Truth: Paul's Ethics in Galatians*. Minneapolis: Fortress, 1991.

Barr, James. *The Concept of Biblical Theology: An Old Testament Perspective*. Minneapolis: Fortress, 1999.

Barth, Markus. *Ephesians 4–6*. AB 34A. New York: Doubleday, 1974.

Bebbington, David W. "Evangelicalism in Its Settings: The British and American Movements since 1940." In *Evangelicalism*, edited by Mark Noll, D. W. Bebbington, and G. A. Rawlyk, 365–88. Oxford: Oxford University Press, 1991.

———. *Evangelicalism in Modern Britain: A History from the 1730s to the 1980s.* London: Unwyn Hyman, 1989.

Best, E. *Ephesians.* ICC. Edinburgh: T&T Clark, 1998.

Bilezikian, G. *Beyond Sex Roles.* 3rd ed. Grand Rapids: Baker Academic, 2006.

Bloesch, Donald. *Essentials of Evangelical Theology.* 2 vols. New York: Harper & Row, 1978.

Bromiley, G., et al., eds. *International Standard Bible Encyclopedia.* Rev. ed. 4 vols. Grand Rapids: Eerdmans, 1979–88.

Brown, Raymond. *The Gospel according to John.* AB. 2 vols. Garden City, NY: Doubleday, 1966, 1970.

Bushnell, Katherine. *God's Word to Women.* 3rd ed. Oakland, CA: private, 1930.

Cervin, R. S. "Does *Kephalē* Mean 'Source' or 'Authority Over' in Greek Literature? A Rebuttal." *TJ*, n.s., 10 (1989): 85–112.

Childs, B. S. *Biblical Theology in Crisis.* Philadelphia: Westminster, 1970.

———. *Biblical Theology of the Old and New Testaments: Theological Reflection on the Christian Bible.* Minneapolis: Fortress, 1992.

Clark, S. B. *Man and Woman in Christ.* Ann Arbor, MI: Servant, 1980.

Coakley, Sarah. *Powers and Submissions.* Oxford: Blackwell, 2002.

Cochran, Pamela. *Evangelical Feminism: A History.* New York: New York University Press, 2004.

Conzelmann, Hans. *1 Corinthians.* Hermeneia. Philadelphia: Fortress, 1975.

Creegan, Nicola H., and Christine D. Pohl. *Living on the Boundaries: Evangelical Women, Feminism, and the Theological Academy.* Downers Grove, IL: InterVarsity, 2005.

Daly, Mary. *The Church and the Second Sex.* New ed. New York: Harper & Row, 1975.

Diodore of Tarsus. *Commentarii in Psalmos, I.* Edited by Jean-Marie Olivier. CCSG 6. Turnhout: Brepols, 1980.

Doughty, Darrell J. "Heiligkeit und Freiheit." PhD diss., University of Göttingen, 1965.

Downie, R. S. *Roles and Values.* London: Methuen, 1971.

Duhem, Pierre. *The Aim and Structure of Physical Theory.* New York: Atheneum, 1981.

Edwards, David, and John Stott. *Evangelical Essentials: A Liberal-Evangelical Dialogue.* Downers Grove, IL: InterVarsity, 1988.

Emmet, Dorothy. *Rules, Roles and Relation.* London: Macmillan, 1966.

Fee, Gordon. *Paul's Letter to the Philippians.* NICNT. Grand Rapids: Eerdmans, 1995.

Fell, Margaret. *A Sincere and Constant Love: An Introduction to the Work of Margaret Fell.* Edited by T. H. S. Wallace. Richmond, IN: Friends United Press, 1992.

Fowl, S. E. "Christology and Ethics in Philippians 2:5–11." In *Where Christology Began: Essays on Philippians 2,* edited by R. P. Martin and B. J. Dodd, 140–53. Louisville: Westminster John Knox, 1998.

———. *The Story of Christ in the Ethics of Paul.* JSNTSup. Sheffield: Sheffield Academic Press, 1990.

Froehlich, Karlfried, ed. *Biblical Interpretation in the Early Church.* Sources of Early Christian Thought. Minneapolis: Fortress, 1984.

Giles, Kevin. *Jesus and the Father: Modern Evangelicals Reinvent the Doctrine of the Trinity*. Grand Rapids: Zondervan, 2006.

———. *The Trinity and Subordinationism: The Doctrine of God and the Contemporary Gender Debate*. Downers Grove, IL: InterVarsity, 2002.

Gill, David W. J. "The Importance of Roman Portraiture for Head Coverings in 1 Corinthians 11:2–16." *TynBul* 41 (1990): 245–60.

Goldstein, Jonathan. *II Maccabees*. AB. New York: Doubleday, 1983.

Green, Joel, and Max Turner, eds. *Between Two Horizons: Spanning New Testament Studies and Systematic Theology*. Grand Rapids: Eerdmans, 2000.

Greenleaf, Robert K. *Servant Leadership*. Mahwah, NJ: Paulist Press, 1977.

———. *The Servant-Leader Within*. Edited by Hamilton Beazley, Julie Beggs, and Larry Spears. Mahwah, NJ: Paulist Press, 2003.

Grenz, Stanley. *Renewing the Center: Evangelical Theology in a Post-theological Era*. 2nd ed. Grand Rapids: Baker Academic, 2006.

Groothuis, Rebecca Merrill. "'Equal in Being, Unequal in Role': Exploring the Logic of Woman's Subordination." In Pierce and Groothuis, *Discovering Biblical Equality*, 301–33.

Grudem, Wayne. *Evangelical Feminism and Biblical Truth*. Sisters, OR: Multnomah, 2004.

Gundry, Patricia. *Woman Be Free! The Clear Message of Scripture*. Grand Rapids: Zondervan, 1977.

Hagner, Donald A. *Matthew 1–13*. WBC. Dallas: Word, 1993.

Hanson, N. R. *Patterns of Discovery*. Cambridge: Cambridge University Press, 1958.

Hauerwas, Stanley. *A Community of Character.* Notre Dame, IN: University of Notre Dame Press, 1981.

Hauerwas, Stanley, and L. G. Jones, eds. *Why Narrative?* Grand Rapids: Eerdmans, 1989.

Hawthorne, G. F. *Philippians.* WBC. Waco: Word, 1983.

Hays, Richard B. *The Moral Vision of the New Testament: A Contemporary Introduction to New Testament Ethics.* San Francisco: HarperSanFrancisco, 1996.

Jewett, P. K. *Man as Male and Female: A Study in Sexual Relationships from a Theological Point of View.* Grand Rapids: Eerdmans, 1975.

Johnson, Alan. "A Christian Understanding of Submission." *PriscPap* 17, no. 4 (Fall 2003): 11–20.

Johnston, Robert K. "American Evangelicalism: An Extended Family." In *The Variety of American Evangelicalism,* edited by D. W. Dayton and R. K. Johnston, 252–72. Knoxville: University of Tennessee Press, 1991.

Kähler, Else. *Die Frau in den paulinischen Briefen.* Zürich: Goffthelf, 1960.

———. "Zur Unterordnung der Frau im Neuen Testament." *ZEE* 3 (1959): 1–13.

Keener, Craig. *Paul, Women and Wives.* Peabody, MA: Hendrickson, 1992.

Knight, George W. *Commentary on the Pastoral Epistles.* NIGTC. Grand Rapids: Eerdmans, 1992.

———. "Male and Female Related He Them." *CT* 20 (April 9, 1976): 13–17.

———. "The New Testament Teaching on the Role Relationship of Male and Female with Special Reference to the Teaching/ Ruling Functions in the Church." *JETS* 18, no. 2 (Spring 1975): 81–91.

————. *The New Testament Teaching on the Role Relationship of Men and Women.* Grand Rapids: Baker Books, 1977.

Kolb, Robert, and Timothy J. Wengert, eds. *The Book of Concord: The Confessions of the Evangelical Lutheran Church.* Minneapolis: Fortress, 2000.

Kuhn, Thomas. *The Structure of Scientific Revolutions.* Chicago: University of Chicago Press, 1970.

Lane, W. L. *The Gospel according to Mark.* NICNT. Grand Rapids: Eerdmans, 1974.

Liddell, H. G., R. Scott, et al. *A Greek-English Lexicon.* 9th ed. Oxford: Oxford University Press, 1983.

Lightfoot, J. B., M. R. Harmer, and M. W. Holmes, eds. *The Apostolic Fathers.* 2nd ed. Grand Rapids: Baker Books, 1992.

Lincoln, A. T. *Ephesians.* WBC. Waco: Word, 1990.

Lippert, Peter. *Leben als Zeugnis.* Stuttgart: Katholisches Bibelwerk, 1968.

Lowrie, Samuel T. "I Corinthians XI and the Ordination of Women as Ruling Elders." *PTR* 19 (1921): 113–30.

Lubac, Henri de. *Medieval Exegesis.* Translated by M. Sebanc and E. M. Macierowski. 4 vols. Grand Rapids: Eerdmans, 1998–2010.

MacIntyre, Alasdair. *After Virtue.* 2nd ed. Notre Dame, IN: University of Notre Dame Press, 1984.

————. *Three Rival Versions of Moral Enquiry.* Notre Dame, IN: University of Notre Dame Press, 1990.

Marsden, George. *Reforming Fundamentalism: Fuller Seminary and the New Evangelicalism.* Grand Rapids: Eerdmans, 1987.

Marshall, I. H. *Commentary on Luke.* NIGTC. Grand Rapids: Eerdmans, 1978.

————. "Mutual Love and Submission in Marriage." In Pierce and Groothuis, *Discovering Biblical Equality*, 186–204.

Martin, Dale. *Slavery as Salvation: The Metaphor of Slavery in Pauline Christianity.* New Haven: Yale University Press, 1990.

Martin, Ralph P. *A Hymn of Christ.* Downers Grove, IL: InterVarsity, 1997.

Marty, Martin E., ed. *Fundamentalism and Evangelicalism.* Munich: K. G. Saur, 1993.

Matheson, Peter. *Argula von Grumbach: A Woman's Voice in the Reformation.* Edinburgh: T&T Clark, 1995.

McKim, Donald, ed. *A Guide to Contemporary Hermeneutics: Major Trends in Biblical Interpretation.* Grand Rapids: Eerdmans, 1986.

Meeks, Wayne A. "The Man from Heaven in Paul's Letter to the Philippians." In *The Future of Early Christianity: Essays in Honor of Helmut Koester*, edited by B. A. Pearson, 329–36. Minneapolis: Fortress, 1991.

Metzger, Bruce M. *A Textual Commentary on the Greek New Testament.* 2nd ed. New York: United Bible Societies, 1994.

Mollenkott, Virginia R. *Women, Men, and the Bible.* Nashville: Abingdon, 1977.

Moule, C. F. D. "Further Reflections on Philippians 2:5–11." In *Apostolic History and the Gospel*, edited by Ralph Martin and Ward Gasque, 264–76. Grand Rapids: Eerdmans, 1970.

Nicene and Post-Nicene Fathers. Edited by Philip Schaff and Henry Wace. 14 vols. Peabody, MA: Hendrickson, 1994.

Noll, Mark. *American Evangelical Christianity: An Introduction.* Oxford: Blackwell, 2001.

Nolland, John. *Luke 1–9:20.* WBC. Dallas: Word, 1989.

Oakley, Justin. *Virtue Ethics and Professional Roles.* Cambridge: Cambridge University Press, 2001.

O'Brien, P. T. *The Letter to the Ephesians.* PNTC. Grand Rapids: Eerdmans, 1999.

O'Collins, G., and D. Kendall. *The Bible for Theology: Ten Principles for the Theological Use of Scripture*. New York: Paulist Press, 1997.

Ollenburger, Ben. "Pursuing the Truth of Scripture." In *But Is It All True? The Bible and the Question of Truth*, edited by Alan G. Padgett and Patrick R. Keifert, 44–65. Grand Rapids: Eerdmans, 2006.

Olson, Roger. *The Westminster Handbook to Evangelical Theology*. Louisville: Westminster John Knox, 2004.

Origen. *Homelies sur la Genese*. SC 7. Edited by Louis Doutreleau. Paris: Cerf, 1976.

———. *Homilies on Genesis and Exodus*. FC 71. Translated by Ronald E. Heine. Washington, DC: Catholic University of America Press, 1982.

Orr, W. F., and J. A. Walther. *I Corinthians*. AB 32. Garden City, NY: Doubleday, 1976.

Padgett, Alan G. "The Canonical Sense of Scripture: Christocentric or Trinitarian?" *Di* 45 (2006): 36–43.

———. "Feminism in First Corinthians: A Dialogue with Elisabeth Schüssler Fiorenza." *EvQ* 58 (1986): 121–32.

———. "Paul on Women in the Church: The Contradictions of Coiffure in 1 Corinthians 11.2–16." *JSNT* 20 (1984): 69–86.

———. "The Pauline Rationale for Submission: Biblical Feminism and the *hina* Clauses of Titus 2:1–10." *EvQ* 59 (1987): 39–52.

———. *Science and the Study of God: A Mutuality Model for Theology and Science*. Grand Rapids: Eerdmans, 2003.

———. "The Significance of ἀντί in 1 Corinthians 11:15." *TynBul* 45 (1994): 181–87.

———. "The Three-fold Sense of Scripture." In *Semper Reformandum: Studies in Honour of Clark H. Pinnock*, edited by S. E. Porter and A. R. Cross, 275–88. Carlisle, UK: Paternoster, 2003.

———. "Wealthy Women at Ephesus: 1 Timothy 2:8–15 in Social Context." *Int* 41 (1987): 19–31.

Palmer, Phoebe. *The Promise of the Father*. Boston: Degan, 1859.

Park, M. Sydney. *Submission within the Godhead and the Church in the Epistle to the Philippians*. London: T&T Clark, 2007.

Perriman, A. "The Head of a Woman." *JTS* 45 (1994): 602–22.

Phelen, James, and P. J. Rabinowitz, eds. *A Companion to Narrative Theory*. Oxford: Blackwell, 2005.

Pierce, Ronald W. "Contemporary Evangelicals for Gender Equality." In Pierce and Groothuis, *Discovering Biblical Equality*, 58–75.

Pierce, Ronald W., and Rebecca Merrill Groothuis, eds. *Discovering Biblical Equality: Complementarity without Hierarchy*. Downers Grove, IL: InterVarsity, 2004.

Piper, John, and Wayne Grudem, eds. *Recovering Biblical Manhood and Womanhood: A Response to Evangelical Feminism*. Wheaton: Crossway, 1991; 2nd ed., 2006.

Polanyi, Michael. *Personal Knowledge: Towards a Post-Critical Philosophy*. Chicago: University of Chicago Press, 1962.

Porter, Stanley. "What Does It Mean to Be 'Saved by Childbirth' (1 Timothy 2:15)?" *JSNT* 49 (1993): 87–102.

Ricoeur, Paul. *Oneself as Another*. Chicago: University of Chicago Press, 1992.

———. *Time and Narrative*. 3 vols. Chicago: University of Chicago Press, 1984–88.

Rudolph, Kurt. *Gnosis: The Nature and History of Gnosticism*. Translated by Robert McLachlan Wilson. San Francisco: Harper & Row, 1983.

Ryrie, C. C. *The Place of Women in the Church*. New York: Macmillan, 1958.

Scanzoni, Letha, and Nancy Hardesty. *All We're Meant to Be: A Biblical Approach to Women's Liberation*. Waco: Word, 1974.

Schneemelcher, W., ed. *New Testament Apocrypha*. 2 vols. Louisville: Westminster John Knox, 1991.

Schrage, W. *The Ethics of the New Testament*. Philadelphia: Fortress, 1988.

Scroggs, Robin. "Paul and the Eschatological Woman." *JAAR* 40 (1972): 283–303.

Smyth, H. W. *Greek Grammar*. Cambridge, MA: Harvard University Press, 1920.

Spencer, Aída Besançon. *Beyond the Curse: Women Called to Ministry*. Nashville: Thomas Nelson, 1985.

———. "Eve at Ephesus." *JETS* 17 (1974): 215–22.

Steinmetz, D. C. "The Superiority of Pre-Critical Exegesis." *ThTo* 37 (1980): 27–38.

Sternberg, Meir. *The Poetics of Biblical Narrative: Ideological Literature and the Drama of Reading*. Bloomington: Indiana University Press, 1985.

Stott, John. *Basic Christianity*. Grand Rapids: Eerdmans, 1971.

Torjesen, Karen Jo. *Hermeneutical Procedure and Theological Method in Origen's Exegesis*. Berlin: de Gruyter, 1985.

Torrance, T. F. *The Trinitarian Faith: The Evangelical Theology of the Ancient Catholic Faith*. Edinburgh: T&T Clark, 1988.

Towner, Peter H. *The Goal of Our Instruction*. Sheffield: Sheffield Academic Press, 1989.

———. *The Letters to Timothy and Titus*. NICNT. Grand Rapids: Eerdmans, 2006.

United Methodist Publishing House. *The Book of Discipline of The United Methodist Church, 2008*. Nashville: United Methodist Publishing House, 2008.

Verhey, Allen. *The Great Reversal: Ethics and the New Testament*. Grand Rapids: Eerdmans, 1988.

Wall, Robert. "Reading the Bible from within Our Traditions: The 'Rule of Faith' in Theological Hermeneutics." In Green and Turner, *Between Two Horizons*, 88–107.

Waters, Kenneth. "Saved through Childbearing: Virtues as Children in 1 Timothy 2:8–15." *JBL* 123 (2004): 703–35.

Watson, Francis. *Text, Church and World*. Edinburgh: T&T Clark, 1994.

———. *Text and Truth: Redefining Biblical Theology*. Edinburgh: T&T Clark, 1997.

Wilkens, S., and A. G. Padgett. *Christianity and Western Thought*. Vol. 2, *A History of Philosophers, Ideas, and Movements*. Downers Grove, IL: InterVarsity, 2000.

Witherington, Ben, III. *The Problem with Evangelical Theology: Testing the Exegetical Foundations of Calvinism, Dispensationalism, and Wesleyanism*. Waco: Baylor University Press, 2005.

Wolterstorff, Nicholas. *Divine Discourse: Philosophical Reflections on the Claim That God Speaks*. Cambridge: Cambridge University Press, 1995.

Wright, N. T. *The Climax of the Covenant*. Edinburgh: T&T Clark, 1991.

Yoder, John H. *The Politics of Jesus*. 2nd ed. Grand Rapids: Eerdmans, 1994.

General Index

allegory, 25–26, 28
allēlois, 41, 44
angels, 112–16
Antiochus V, 40
Aristotle, 24, 34n4, 63

Barth, Karl, 23
Basil the Great, 26
Bebbington, David W., 16
biblical equality, 5, 8, 10–13, 13n18, 59n2
biblical feminism, 7–8
Bilezikian, Gilbert, 39
body of Christ, 40, 49, 73, 110, 127. *See also* church

Cervin, Richard, 66
character, 13, 16, 18, 23, 32–37, 46–49, 71, 88, 91. *See also* vice; virtue
Childs, B. S., 22, 22n30, 23n34
Christ. *See* Jesus Christ
Christ-centered, 2–3, 11, 17–19, 28–29, 56, 68–69, 82
Christian feminism, 5–7, 10–11
Christians for Biblical Equality, 11, 11n15
church, 1–2, 4–11, 13–14, 16–26, 28–30, 32, 35, 41, 44–46, 48, 55, 58–60, 62–73, 75–77, 81, 84–85, 87, 89, 91, 94–97, 99–101, 106–7, 109, 111–13, 119–20, 122–23, 125–28, 130

community, 3, 18, 20–24, 28–29, 36–37, 61, 80, 82, 86, 101, 127, 131
complementarian, 2, 5, 10–13, 15, 32–33, 39, 43, 51, 98, 100
Constantine, 125
Council on Biblical Manhood and Womanhood, 10, 12–13
creation-order, 58, 77, 88–89

Daly, Mary, 4
de Lubac, Henri, 26
Diodore of Taurus, 22, 25

egalitarian, 9–12, 14, 39, 43, 51, 69–71
empire, 81, 83, 85, 100, 126
Epiphanes, Antiochus IV, 40
evangelical, 1–19, 22–23, 25–28, 30–31, 37, 45, 51, 56–57, 82–83, 87, 126–127, 129
Evangelical and Ecumenical Women's Caucus, 8n11, 11
evangelical theology, 15–17, 16nn20–22
Evangelical Women's Caucus, 8, 8n11, 11
exegesis, 3, 14, 23, 25–26, 91, 117
exousia, 43, 67, 112

feminism, 6–7, 10, 12
Fowl, Stephen, 47
Fox, Margaret Fell, 5

145

Scripture Index

149